OSPREY AIRCRAFT OF THE ACES • 85

Ki-43 'Oscar' Aces
of World War 2

SERIES EDITOR: TONY HOLMES

OSPREY AIRCRAFT OF THE ACES • 85

Ki-43 'Oscar' Aces of World War 2

Hiroshi Ichimura

OSPREY
PUBLISHING

Front Cover
On 27 March 1943, RAF Hurricane IIs from Nos 79 and 135 Sqns succeeded in shooting down no fewer than five Japanese Army Air Force (JAAF) Kawasaki Ki-48 'Lily' light bombers without loss over Cox's Bazaar, in what was then eastern India. A force of 25 Ki-48s had been despatched to attack Allied targets along the Arakan coast, and these aircraft should have been escorted by Ki-43-II 'Oscars' from the 50th Sentai. However, the fighters had failed to arrive at their rendezvous point so the bombers pressed on alone.

Anxious to restore its reputation following this debacle, the 50th Sentai sought swift revenge for its fallen comrades. The opportunity came on 31 March, when eight hand-picked combat veterans (all of whom would ultimately become 'Oscar' aces) from the sentai, led by their commanding officer, Maj Tadashi Ishikawa, departed the unit's base at Meiktila soon after dawn and attacked the advanced Allied airfield at Pataga. Having made their strafing runs, the 'Oscar' pilots then climbed to 19,000 ft east of Buthidaung and formed up into a formation dubbed the 'beehive' by RAF pilots. Keen for a fight, the JAAF pilots moved steadily southward, enticing the ten Hurricane pilots from No 135 Sqn that had been scrambled to intercept them to head deeper into Japanese-held territory.

Using their superior height and speed, the 'Oscar' pilots bounced the RAF fighters as they climbed up through the heavy mist that blanketed the area. In the fierce dogfight that ensued, the 50th Sentai claimed to have shot down eight Hurricanes and probably destroyed six more – the Ki-43 pilots reported that they had engaged no fewer than 40 Hurricanes and P-40s! Three RAF fighters had actually been destroyed, with a fourth machine badly shot up. Two pilots had been killed and two more wounded.

Despite having suffered varying degrees of battle damage, all the Ki-43s returned to base. Future eight-kill ace, and 2nd Chutai leader, Capt Masao Miyamaru, who is seen here finishing off a Hurricane, claimed three kills, and his wingman, Sgt Yukio Shimokawa (who would eventually achieve a score of 16), was credited with downing two of the British fighters (*Cover artwork by Mark Postlethwaite*)

First published in Great Britain in 2009 by Osprey Publishing
Midland House, West Way, Botley, Oxford, OX2 0PH
443 Park Avenue South, New York, NY, 10016, USA
E-mail; info@ospreypublishing.com

Print ISBN: 978 1 84603 408 4
PDF e-book ISBN: 978 1 84603 861 7

Edited by Bruce Hales-Dutton and Tony Holmes
Page design by Tony Truscott
Cover Artwork by Mark Postlethwaite
Line drawings by Mark Styling
Aircraft Profiles by Jim Laurier
Originated by United Graphics Pte
Index by Alan Thatcher
Printed and bound in China through Bookbuilders

09 10 11 12 13   10 9 8 7 6 5 4 3 2 1

For a catalogue of all books published by Osprey please contact:

North America
Osprey Direct, C/o Random House Distribution Center,
400 Hahn Road, Westminster, MD 21157
E-mail: uscustomerservice@ospreypublishing.com

All Other Regions
Osprey Direct, The Book Service Ltd, Distribution Centre, Colchester Road, Frating Green, Colchester, Essex, CO7 7DW, UK
E-mail: customerservice@ospreypublishing.com

Osprey Publishing is supporting the Woodland Trust, the UK's leading woodland conservation charity, by funding the dedication of trees.

www.ospreypublishing.com

CONTENTS

A DIFFICULT START

It was a day Lt Ichiro Niimi would never forget. The young engineer was in charge of the groundcrew tending the 12 Ki-43 Type 1 Army fighters of the Japanese Army Air Force's 3rd Chutai/64th Sentai, based at Duong Dong airfield on Idu Phu Quoc, off the coast of Japanese-occupied French Indochina. The date was 7 December 1941, and World War 2 was about to explode across Asia and the Pacific region. Decades later, Niimi recalled, 'When all 35 of our Ki-43s fired up their engines for a test run at dawn, the thundering sound had me shaking with anticipation. We then test fired our guns over the ocean'.

The fighter's forthcoming debut in combat with the Western allies had not always been so keenly anticipated. Indeed, the majority of JAAF pilots had initially viewed the new machine with deep suspicion, and were reluctant to exchange it for their agile Ki-27 Type 97s. The 64th Sentai pilots were no exception. 'The new fighter is huge, and it has retractable landing gear' was Niimi's reaction when he saw the Ki-43 for the first time at Fussa airfield, near Tokyo, in September 1941.

But replacement of the tried and combat-tested, but obsolete, Ki-27 that JAAF fighter pilots had achieved so much success with over China in 1938-39 was considered essential for the coming war, as it was expected that future operations would see aircraft flying much longer distances.

By this time the new fighter had already started to acquire a dubious reputation for more than just teething troubles. Within a month of being re-equipped with 30 Ki-43-Ias in June-August 1941, Sgt Inamura of the 59th Sentai (the first unit to receive the Nakajima fighter) was forced to bale out of his Model I-Ko (A) when it failed to recover from a spin during combat training. The remains of the crashed aircraft were recovered and investigators discovered that the wings folded at the roots.

The JAAF was reluctant to take drastic action to remedy this obvious structural defect, however. Time was pressing, and the aircraft, with its enhanced capability, was urgently needed in China. The 59th was sent to Hankow in the autumn of 1941, from where nine aircraft, led by Capt Akera, participated in a long-range raid on Chonging. This mission represented the Ki-43's combat debut, but the Chinese declined to engage the new fighters, having already learned a hard lesson in combat with the Imperial Japanese Navy's new A6M2 Zero-Sen. Despite having seen no aerial combat, the Ki-43 had more than proven its long-range capabilities.

By then, the most famous of all JAAF units to operate the Ki-43 had swapped its Ki-27s for the new Nakajima fighter. The 64th Sentai had claimed 97 aerial victories in China and 52 during the Nomonhan Incident, thus making it one of the

The 64th Sentai was equipped with the simple and reliable Ki-27 between April 1938 and November 1941, when the last examples were replaced by Ki-43-Is. Noteworthy in this photograph is the sentai's red eagle insignia displayed below the fighter's cockpit, as well as the all-red cowling that denotes the Ki-27's assignment to the 1st Chutai. Nineteen future Ki-43 aces scored victories in the Ki-27 over China in 1938-39 (*64th Sentai Association*)

more successful fighter units in the JAAF by the end of 1939. The sentai would subsequently see considerable action in the Greater East Asian War under the leadership of Maj Tateo Kato, who would become the most famous of all JAAF fighter pilots during his six months in combat. Having claimed 28 aerial victories (including ten in China in 1937-38) by the time of his death in action on 22 May 1942, Kato was posthumously awarded the accolade of 'God of the Clouds' by a grateful nation, and his sentai would become the source of many Ki-43 aces.

Kato's 64th Sentai (with the 3rd Chutai led by future 12-victory ace Capt Katsumi Anma) arrived at Fussa from Canton, on the South China front, in late August 1941 and immediately commenced its conversion to the Ki-43-Ia. It suffered its first loss with the new aircraft on 19 October, when veteran pilot Sgt Maj Saburo Seki was killed during a mock dogfight. He was unable to pull out of a steep dive after the wings of his fighter suffered catastrophic structural failure.

The 64th Sentai's remaining Ki-43-Ias were hastily checked following this accident, and the groundcrew were alarmed to find cracks around wheel wells and wrinkling of the skin covering the wing roots. JAAF headquarters recalled all Ki-43-Is assigned to the 59th and 64th Sentais, and these were sent to the Nakajima factory at Ojima airfield.

Having exploited the Ki-27's agility over China, JAAF pilots had demanded that its replacement be as light and manoeuvrable as possible. However, the Army had instructed Nakajima to incorporate a retractable undercarriage into its design. The new fighter also had to be capable of achieving speeds in excess of 500 kmh, attain an altitude of 5000 m in five minutes and boast a range of 800 km. Essentially, the JAAF wanted an aircraft that was as agile as the Ki-27, but with a higher top speed and longer range. Nakajima struggled with these requirements, and the prototype weighed 1900 kg, compared to 1790 kg for the Ki-27. The new machine was also larger in dimension. Following its maiden flight on 12 December 1938, the fighter was test flown at the Keno Flying School, where it was found to be inferior to the Ki-27 in a horizontal dogfight.

Nakajima shed weight from the airframe in an effort to boost the Ki-43's agility, but by doing this it compromised the fighter's structural integrity. Nevertheless, the aircraft was selected for production in April 1941 as a long-range fighter escort. By then, Nakajima had incorporated innovative 'butterfly' flaps into the Ki-43's revised wing shape, and the end result was an aircraft that could beat the Ki-27 in a turning fight.

It was only once the initial production Ki-43-Ias began to reach frontline units in the summer of 1941 that problems with the fighter's build quality began to surface. Following the failures detailed earlier in this chapter, all surviving aircraft were returned to Nakajima so that their wing roots could be strengthened. The company took this opportunity to install plumbing that would allow the Ki-43-I to carry drop-tanks too.

The initial production version (Model IA) had been armed with two nose-mounted 7.7 mm Type 89 machine guns, but when production switched to the Model IB in late 1941, the left-hand gun was replaced by a 12.7 mm calibre Ho-103 weapon. This was classified as a cannon by the JAAF because it fired an explosive shell. Nakajima had intended to replace both rifle-calibre guns, but there had been instances of early production shells exploding before or just after leaving the muzzle. Jams

The 64th Sentai's charismatic commander, Maj Tateo Kato, would become the best-known JAAF fighter pilot of World War 2 when he and his unit engaged Allied air forces in South East Asia in 1941-42. This photograph of the Nomonhan Incident ace was taken at the sentai's Canton base shortly before the commencement of the Greater East Asian War (*64th Sentai Association*)

were also frequent. Despite these problems, JAAF pilots were eager to use the weapon, and the initial solution was to keep one 7.7 mm gun as a back-up. These modified Ki-43s were designated as the Model I Otsu (B).

Once cleared for operational use, the first examples of strengthened Ki-43-Ibs were reissued to the 64th Sentai in early November 1941. The unit returned to Canton shortly afterwards. Prior to his departure, Maj Kato requested permission from JAAF Headquarters for his aircraft to have two Ho-103 cannon fitted, and for the others in his unit to be so equipped if the installation in his machine proved trouble-free.

Although the distance from Fussa to Canton was some 2000 km, pilots from the 64th had been well prepared for the return flight by their CO. Kato, who was fully aware of why the Ki-43 had been adopted for service by the JAAF, had stressed training in over-sea navigation and long distance flights prior to the unit heading back to China. These sorties paid off, for all the pilots in his sentai successfully completed the journey.

Although the wing strengthening had solved some of the structural problems that had afflicted early Ki-43s, the 64th Sentai soon discovered more skin wrinkling around the wing roots with the commencement of air combat training in China. Pilots immediately lost confidence in their new mounts, but Kato was undaunted. 'We had no choice but to fly in the same way as Maj Kato', recalled a Ki-43 pilot from the 64th Sentai.

Despite these problems, the JAAF declared the Ki-43 ready for battle, although only two sentais – the 59th and 64th – had re-equipped with the new Nakajima fighter prior to the outbreak of war in this theatre.

As part of the Japanese High Command's preparation for the Greater East Asian War, the JAAF's two Ki-43 units were moved from China to Duong Dong airfield, on Idu Phu Quoc, on 3 December. The 64th Sentai fielded 35 Ki-43-Ibs and the 59th had 21. The units would be charged with providing long range fighter cover for the 18 troop-laden transport vessels in which Gen Tomoyuki Yamashita's 25th Army – designated 'Force Malaya' – was embarked.

For several days the units flew patrols over the invasion fleet as it headed for Malaya, and these missions proved uneventful until dusk on 7 December, when three Ki-43s from the 64th Sentai failed to return to base after becoming lost in fog and cloud.

The invasion of the Malayan Peninsula began in the early hours of 8 December, and the Ki-43s were heavily involved in escorting JAAF heavy bombers sent to attack key Allied targets. The fighters also strafed various airfields during the course of the day, and five aircraft were credited to the 64th Sentai as destroyed on the ground. The unit also claimed the first aerial victory with the Ki-43 when three of its pilots (including future 12-kill ace 1Lt Yohei Hinoki) shared in the destruction of a Blenheim IV from No 34 Sqn that was attacking landing barges near Ayer Tawar.

Two more Blenheim IVs from this unit were attacked by fighters from the 59th Sentai as the bombers attempted to land at Butterworth to refuel following the raid on the invasion beachhead. With two victories from the Nomonhan Incident already to his name, veteran fighter pilot (and future nine-kill ace) WO Takeomi Hayashi was credited with destroying both Blenheim IVs, thus claiming his unit's first kills with the Ki-43.

The 59th also escorted light bombers sent to attack Kota Bharu airfield, and as the formation approached Tanah Merah, it was reportedly

This Ki-43-I of the 64th Sentai's 2nd Chutai was assigned to Lt Yohei Hinoki, who was to become an ace during the fighting in Malaya and the East Indies. Note that this aircraft has been fitted with a single 200-litre drop tank beneath its port wing. The fighter's telescopic gunsight is also clearly visible, this equipment being identical to the sight fitted to the Ki-27. Most other frontline fighters on either side were fitted with the more modern, and effective, reflector gunsight, and Allied pilots would take advantage of the Ki-43's telescopic sight to effect their escape. Burma Hurricane pilot Sgt Bob Windle recalled 'All the Ki-43s we encountered in 1942 were fitted with an Aldis Sight method of aiming their guns, which required the pilot to get his eye close to the telescopic type sight in order to aim his guns. This proved fatal to many Japanese pilots when trying to aim at an Allied aircraft when close to the ground in a hilly or wooded area. We were fully aware of this, and had been ordered to "hit the deck and take evasive action" should a Ki-43 get on our tail' (*64th Sentai Association*)

intercepted by Buffalo fighters. The Ki-43 pilots claimed six of the Allied fighters shot down, but this action cannot be reconciled with RAF or RAAF losses on this date.

Three Ki-43s had been lost on the opening day of the Greater East Asian War, with two from the 59th Sentai crashing in bad weather and a single machine from the 64th Sentai ditching off Idu Phu Quoc after being hit in error by anti-aircraft fire from a Japanese destroyer.

On the 9th, both Ki-43 units undertook more strafing attacks in support of the Japanese advance on the ground. Two days later, the 64th moved to the newly captured airfield at Kota Bharu as the invasion of northern Malaya proceeded as planned – the unit replenished its fighters with fuel taken from abandoned RAF aircraft. Bomber escort missions continued to keep all JAAF fighter sentais busy, although few Allied fighters were encountered in the wake of the devastating airfield attacks of 8 December. On the 12th, the 59th Sentai transferred 20 of its Ki-43s to Nakhorn, in Thailand, and it suffered a terrible blow just 24 hours later when its CO, Maj Reinosuke Tanimura, perished in a mid-air collision.

Having led his unit in a strafing attack on Butterworth, which saw four Buffaloes destroyed, Tanimura hit his wingman's Ki-43 during the return flight to Nakhorn and crashed to his death. Tanimura's aircraft was one of ten Ki-43s lost to all causes between 8 and 15 December.

As Japanese troops pushed south towards Singapore, the airfield at Ipoh, on the west coast of Malaya, was increasingly targeted by the JAAF. On 16 December, three Australian Buffaloes and an identical number of Ki-43s from the 59th Sentai clashed directly overhead the base as the latter attempted to conduct a strafing attack. The RAAF aircraft were totally outfought, although none were shot down – despite claims by JAAF pilots that they had destroyed two of the *six* Buffaloes encountered!

More strafing attacks were made on Ipoh over the next few days, and the 59th Sentai succeeded in downing a Buffalo on the 21st whilst escorting Ki-48s and Ki-51s sent to bomb the airfield in Kuala Lumpur. Two fighters from No 453 Sqn RAAF had been conducting an airfield patrol at the time, and while one went after the bombers the other Buffalo kept the fighters busy. It was the latter aircraft that was duly downed, although the sentai claimed four destroyed. Amongst the pilots credited with a kill was future 14-victory ace Capt Hiroshi Onozaki.

On 22 December it was the turn of the 64th Sentai to engage the Buffaloes of No 453 Sqn in what turned out to be the biggest aerial battle of the Malayan campaign to date. Twelve RAAF fighters had scrambled from Kuala Lumpur at 1000 hrs, and these aircraft had initially been engaged by six Ki-43s at 7000 ft. A further dozen Japanese fighters then joined the melee. According to a contemporary JAAF report, 'Advanced attack formations of the 2nd Chutai, led by Lt Tadao Takayama, sighted 15 or 16 Buffaloes below them. Takayama waggled his wings, thus signalling "Tally ho!" to his pilots'.

Amongst those arriving on the scene shortly after Takayama had attacked the Australian fighters was future 12-kill ace Sgt Maj Yoshito Yasuda, who was about to get his first taste of aerial combat. He recalled;

'Ki-43s of the attack formations turned one by one and chased the enemy – I soon saw two parachutes. Our support formations from the 3rd Chutai, led by Capt Katsumi Anma, waited ten to twenty seconds before we attacked. I was Capt Anma's wingman, and by the time we dived into the combat zone, there seemed to be no enemy aircraft around for us to go after. Luckily, Anma found a fleeing Buffalo and attacked it from above and behind. My turn came when Anma's guns jammed. I sent a burst into the Buffalo and saw it belch white smoke. I could not confirm that it crashed, however.'

The dogfight had lasted more than 30 minutes when the 64th Sentai broke off the engagement due to a shortage of fuel. Upon returning to Kota Bharu, pilots claimed 11 confirmed and four probable victories, although in reality only three Buffaloes had been shot down and two more forced to crash-land. Two RAAF pilots were killed and two wounded, and No 453 Sqn had in turn been credited with the destruction of three Ki-43s, plus six probables.

The only loss suffered by the 64th Sentai was 2nd Chutai leader Lt Takayama. His wingman, Sgt Maj Okuyama, reported that Takayama's Ki-43 had been damaged by anti-aircraft fire at the start of the encounter, but that he had downed three Buffaloes nevertheless, and then dived after another that he spotted fleeing from the scene at very low altitude. Although Takayama was seen to close in on the RAAF fighter, he did not open fire, and in the next moment the two aircraft exploded. Takayama had either rammed the enemy machine after his guns had jammed or his fighter had disintegrated when he pulled out after diving on the Buffalo.

Takayama's demise matches up with the RAAF loss report for Sgt Mac Read, which states that the latter pilot 'was killed having been last seen apparently ramming or crashing into an opponent as he went down in Buffalo W8209/F'.

Although 64th Sentai CO Maj Kato had witnessed the incident, and judged that Takayama had been the victim of the Ki-43's frail construction, it was later depicted as a ramming in the 1944 propaganda film *Kato Hayabusa Sento-tai*, which detailed the exploits of Kato and his unit.

Upon landing after the battle, Kato ordered an inspection of all of his unit's Ki-43s. Again, wrinkles and cracks were found in the wing skins around the wheel wells in six aircraft. Soon afterwards, Kato flew to Sungai Petani airfield to report the matter to JAAF engineers, who had recently arrived from Japan. He implored them to remedy the aircraft's weak construction and frequent gun jams, and temporary repairs were made to the affected aircraft at the frontline workshop at Kota Bharu.

Amongst the pilots credited with victories on the 22nd were future aces 1Lts Yohei Hinoki and Shogo Takeuchi and Sgts Yoshito Yasuda and Miyoshi Watanabe.

Several hours after the 64th Sentai had clashed with No 453 Sqn, it was the turn of the 59th Sentai to attack Kuala Lumpur. Four Ki-43s strafed the airfield just as all the available Buffaloes were ordered to scramble. Only one RAAF fighter managed to get airborne, and it was quickly shot down.

Nomonhan ace Capt Katsumi Anma was leader of the 64th Sentai's 3rd Chutai from September 1940 until he was killed in combat fighting the AVG on 8 April 1942. A close and trusted friend of Maj Kato, Anma had added seven aerial victories in the Ki-43 to the five he had scored in China by the time of his death (*64th Sentai Association*)

The 64th Sentai's 2nd Chutai lost its leader, Capt Tadao Takayama, in combat with RAAF Buffaloes on 22 December 1941 (*64th Sentai Association*)

On 24 December the 64th Sentai was transferred to Don Muang airfield, near Bangkok, following the loss of five Ki-21s during a raid on the Burmese capital of Rangoon the previous day. These aircraft had been escorted by Ki-27s from the 77th Sentai, but the JAAF fighters were unable to prevent the P-40Bs of the American Volunteer Group (AVG) from attacking the bombers. It was hoped that the faster Ki-43s would provide better protection to the vulnerable Ki-21s.

The Christmas Day attack was to be the biggest raid to date on Rangoon. A total of 25 Ki-43s were charged with escorting 63 Ki-21s from the 7th Flying Battalion, this formation being followed by eight Ki-21s and 27 Ki-30s from the 10th Flying Battalion – the latter were escorted by 32 Ki-27s from the 77th Sentai.

Kato explained the importance of this mission to his men prior to their departure from Don Muang, telling them that 'We must drive away the enemy fighters from our bombers like a paper fan against flies'. However, 24 of his pilots forgot the instruction to protect the bombers when challenged by 14 Buffaloes from No 67 Sqn and 12 AVG P-40Bs. Only Kato stuck with the bombers, which were badly mauled by the Allied fighters. The 12th Sentai lost three Ki-21s, and a fourth bomber crash-landed upon its return to base.

Chasing after the P-40Bs and Buffaloes, the Ki-43 pilots lodged claims for ten fighters destroyed (two P-40Bs and four Buffaloes were actually shot down, with two of the latter badly damaged) for the loss of two Ki-43s and their pilots, including Lt Hiroshi Okumura, whose aircraft collided with the P-40B flown by Parker Dupouy. The wings of the Japanese fighter folded up and the Ki-43 crashed, although the P-40 that it hit lost only its wingtip and Dupouy was able to land safely.

Kato, who had single-handedly escorted a sentai of Ki-21s to and from Rangoon, raged at his pilots for ignoring his orders. He would have been incandescent with rage had he known that not a single Allied fighter had fallen to a Ki-43. Both JAAF and RAF combat records suggest that most of the Allied losses had been inflicted by the Ki-27s of the 77th Sentai. The only possible victory attributable to the 64th was Ed Overend's P-40B, which was damaged by Kato and forced to make a wheels-up landing in a dry rice paddy, while Lt Yohei Hinoki might have damaged the Buffalo flown by Plt Off G S Sharp.

The 64th Sentai rejoined the 59th Sentai at Kota Bharu shortly after this mission. The latter unit would claim the next kills credited to the Ki-43 on New Year's Day, when two Blenheim Is from No 62 Sqn and a Dutch Martin 139WH-3 of 1-VlG-III were downed whilst trying to attack Japanese motor launches operating on the Bernam River. These successes took the 59th's tally to 11 aerial and 13 strafing victories since combat had commenced on 8 December. It had lost just two pilots during the same period.

Capt Tadao Takayama taxies out in his Ki-43-I at Kota Bharu at the start of the fateful sortie that would ultimately result in his death. The chutai leader lost his life either colliding with a Buffalo from No 453 Sqn or suffering catastrophic wing failure whilst attempting to pull up after attacking an RAAF fighter. The Ki-43-I may have also been hit in the tail section by machine gun rounds fired from another Buffalo (*64th Sentai Association*)

After two weeks of relative inactivity, the 64th Sentai moved to Ipoh, on the west coast of Malaya, on 9 January 1942 so as to be closer to the action. The 59th Sentai, meanwhile, had been posted to Sungei Patani, north of Ipoh.

By 11 January Kuala Lumpur had fallen to the Japanese, and the following day the JAAF began its bombing offensive against fortress Singapore. Nearly all JAAF units committed to the Greater East Asian War were now based in northern and central Malaya, ready for the campaign against Allied forces crowded onto Singapore island. No fewer than 42 Ki-43s from both sentais would be tasked with escorting 30 bombers from the 7th Flying Battalion on 12 January – the first day of the Singapore offensive. Things got off to bad start for the 59th when one of its aircraft collided with three others on take-off and all four machines were lost, as were two of the pilots.

The fighter units found little in the way of opposition over Singapore, and only a single Blenheim I of No 34 Sqn was claimed to have been shot down. A number of Ki-43 pilots also fleetingly engaged Buffaloes during the course of the mission, but no meaningful results were achieved by either side. One of the Allied pilots to tangle with the JAAF fighters was future Buffalo ace Sgt Geoff Fisken of No 243 Sqn. He managed to down a Ki-27, but found that the Ki-43s were much harder to beat. In Fisken's combat account from this mission, the New Zealander makes the common mistake of identifying the Ki-43 as an A6M2 Zero-sen;

'The "Zero" and the Buffalo were miles apart. The "Zero" could out-pace, out-climb and out-manoeuvre the Buffalo, but could not out-dive it. To go into a "Zero" on even terms or at a slight disadvantage was literally committing suicide, and after a few early lessons when in that position, you turned over onto your back and dived for the deck.

'In one of my first encounters I put my undercarriage and flaps fully down – I remember thinking I'd hit a brick wall, but I did manage to turn inside the "Zero" and give him a burst of a few seconds. I didn't wait to see the result as there were plenty of Japs around.'

Ki-43s from the 59th Sentai next fought Buffaloes from several RAF and RNZAF units on 15 January when the JAAF fighters escorted 16 bombers sent to attack the airfield at Tengah and the naval base at Sembawang. Pilots claimed six Buffaloes shot down, although only two were actually lost at most and a number of others damaged.

The 64th Sentai was also in action that same day, escorting bombers sent to attack Seletar and Singapore City. A solitary Ki-43 from the unit was damaged when a 12.7 mm round prematurely exploded during a strafing pass at Seletar. Its pilot, Sgt Maj Kondo, force-landed near Kelong whilst attempting to make it back to Ipoh. Worse was to come 48 hours later.

On 17 January, three Ki-43s were brought down by exploding ammunition, although this time the

Seen at a Malayan airfield in late 1941, this 64th Sentai Ki-43-I has its Nakajima Ha-25 950 hp 14-cylinder radial engine test run following maintenance by 1st Chutai groundcrewmen. The Ki-43 was rarely flown without the propeller spinner in place (*64th Sentai Association*)

aircraft were also attacked by Australian Buffaloes. Maj Kato had led pilots from the 64th Sentai's 1st and 2nd Chutais on a strafing mission to Sumatra's Pakan Baroe airfield. During the course of the operation nine RAF Vildebeest biplane bombers were spotted attacking landing barges off Singapore's Johore coast. They were escorted by RAAF Buffaloes, which bounced the Ki-43s as they attempted to attack the Vildebeests.

Maj Kato's Korean-born wingman Lt Takeshi Takeyama had just opened fire at a Vildebeest when a 12.7 mm shell exploded as it emerged from the gun muzzle, badly damaging the Ki-43's engine. The pilot crash-landed near Lake Pakan Baroe. Setting fire to his fighter, Takeyama exchanged shots with Allied troops who had been attracted by the smoke, before committing suicide with the last bullet in his pistol.

Lt Rokuzo, who was the 2nd Chutai leader, also experienced an exploding round whilst attacking Pakan Baroe airfield. His wingman, Cpl Sato, later reported that Rokuzo's face had been covered with oil from the damaged engine of his fighter. He elected to crash to his death in his crippled Ki-43 rather than risk being taken prisoner. Finally, Sgt Maj Saito was assumed to have fallen victim to premature shell detonation as well when he failed to return to Ipoh.

64th Sentai engineer Lt Ichiro Niimi recalled how his unit was often plagued by technical maladies during the early months of the Greater East Asian War;

'The new aircraft had plenty of problems, with the premature detonation of the 12.7 mm rounds being one of the worst. They were supposed to explode when they hit their target, but they often went off just after they left the muzzle, directly over the engine. This was a very serious problem, and in order to correct it, groundcrews had to attach 5 mm thick protective steel plates beneath the muzzles. This modification took 24 hours to complete.'

On a more positive note, the rubber covering fitted to the Ki-43's fuel tanks had been shown to provide the aircraft with a degree of fire prevention, albeit inferior to that of Allied aircraft, in combat conditions. Japanese engineers had, however, encountered difficulty with bonding the two layers of rubber to confer effective sealing in tropical conditions.

The ongoing problems that the 64th Sentai was experiencing with exploding ammunition did not stop future nine-kill ace Sgt Maj Shokichi Omori and Lt Masabumi Kunii from claiming four RAF Catalinas

Sgt Kohei Shoji, who was a senior member of Lt Yohei Hinoki's groundcrew, sits beneath the wing of a 64th Sentai/2nd Chutai Ki-43-I at Ipoh airfield, in Malaya, in late January 1942. Capt Anma, Lt Niimi and other sentai pilots had had their groundcrews apply the 64th's arrow marking to their new aircraft when they converted from the Ki-27 to the Ki-43 in the autumn of 1941. The unit's chutai arrow colours were white for the 1st, red for the 2nd and yellow for the 3rd, with cobalt denoting fighters assigned to the HQ flight (*64th Sentai Association*)

destroyed on the water during a strafing attack on the flying boat anchorage at Seletar on 17 January.

It was the 59th Sentai's turn to see action the following day, when four aircraft led by Maj Hirobuni Muta intercepted three Blenheim Is of No 34 Sqn over the west coast of Johore. One was shot down and a second forced to crash-land at Tengah. A short while later, Muta and his pilots engaged three RAAF Hudsons and two Buffaloes that were attempting to attack Japanese landing barges in the Muar River. One Buffalo was quickly shot down and two of the Hudsons badly damaged – one later crashed as it approached the airfield at Sembawang.

The 3rd Chutai of the 64th Sentai also saw action on 18 January whilst escorting Ki-21s of the 7th Flying Battalion. A dozen Buffaloes from Nos 243 and 488 Sqns were bounced at 16,000 ft over Singapore as they attempted to attack the bombers, and during the one-sided dogfight that ensued, the JAAF pilots claimed to have shot all of them down (two were credited to Lt Masabumi Kunii). Two Buffaloes were indeed destroyed, with a further five badly damaged.

The 59th Sentai saw considerable action on the 19th, downing an RAAF Buffalo that was attacking a Ki-51 near Batu Pahat. Several hours later, a patrol of Ki-43s spotted three unescorted Dutch Martin 139WH-3 bombers heading back to Singapore after bombing an Army HQ. One was shot down and the remaining two were forced to crash-land. Finally, Maj Muta led yet another successful attack against nine Australian and New Zealand Buffaloes over Batu Pahat, the 20 Ki-43 pilots being credited with downing four fighters (two No 488 Sqn aircraft were destroyed) after bouncing them at low-level. One JAAF fighter was lost in return.

Ki-43s encountered Hurricanes for the first time on the morning of 20 January when the 64th Sentai and No 232 Sqn met overhead Singapore. The JAAF fighters were escorting Ki-21s sent to bomb the Hurricane unit's base at Seletar as part of the biggest raid to date on the embattled island. Flying one of the Nakajima fighters was Lt Yonesaku Hatta, who had woken his friend Lt Yohei Hinoki earlier that day with the news, 'I've snapped my toothbrush. I will die today'. Hinoki laughed this gloomy premonition away, but he was to remember it several hours later.

The Hurricanes had arrived in Singapore three days earlier, and they carried the hopes of the hard-pressed defenders into action that morning. Having reached 28,000 ft, the 12 RAF fighters were ordered by Ground Control to attack the 80+ bombers that were some 8000 ft below them. The unit peeled off to intercept the seemingly unescorted aircraft, but had missed the call that there were Japanese fighters above the bombers at 22,000 ft. Maj Kato saw the Hurricanes diving down and immediately climbed up to engage them.

Lt Endo was the first to fire at a Hurricane, but he missed in his excitement. He then spotted another formation just below him. Endo watched as a Ki-43 turned towards the five RAF fighters, waggling its wings as its pilot signalled an attack. It dived on one of the Hurricanes, and after a six-second burst of cannon fire, the British machine belched flame. Endo then saw a white parachute canopy. He also noticed the slanting white line on the wings of the attacking Ki-43, indicating that it was Maj Kato's machine.

Close friends Lts Yonesaku Hatta (right) and Yohei Hinoki of the 64th Sentai. On the morning of 20 January 1942, Hatta took a broken toothbrush to be an ill omen (*Yasuho Izawa*)

In just a matter of minutes the 64th Sentai claimed five Hurricanes for the loss of one Ki-43 and its pilot – Lt Hatta, who had earlier foreseen his own death. Having shot down the lead Hurricane flown by Sqn Ldr Leslie Landels, he had then been attacked by future ace Plt Off 'Jimmy' Parker. Lt Kato tried to warn Hatta, but his radio (another unreliable feature of the Ki-43 at that time) was malfunctioning. Hatta's stricken fighter plunged into the sea. The RAF had actually lost three Hurricanes in the encounter.

In the final action involving Ki-43s on the 20th, three 59th Sentai machines were scrambled from Ipoh to intercept Blenheims from No 34 Sqn that had attacked Kuala Lumpur airfield shortly after sunset. Maj Muta and Lt Shohei Inaba downed one between them, and Muta also claimed a second probably destroyed – the latter machine crash-landed upon its return to Tengah.

The 64th Sentai was in action again the following day when it tangled with Buffaloes from No 243 Sqn and Hurricanes from No 232 Sqn. The Ki-43 pilots claimed a total of six RAF fighters destroyed, with a single aircraft lost in return. The 64th found itself in the thick of things once again on 23 January, claiming more Buffaloes and Hurricanes destroyed for a single Ki-43 shot down.

With fewer and fewer Allied aircraft now appearing in the skies over Malaya and Singapore, and the recent arrival of IJN land- and carrier-based fighter units in-theatre, JAAF fighter pilots found it increasingly difficult to add further victories to their growing tallies. Nevertheless, on 29 January ace Sgt Maj Shokichi Omori claimed two kills when he intercepted Buffaloes and Hurricanes whilst escorting bombers sent to attack Sembawang.

The siege of Singapore began on 31 January, and the 64th Sentai clashed with newly arrived Hurricane unit No 258 Sqn as the latter went after 27 JAAF bombers sent to attack Tengah airfield. The Japanese fighter pilots reported intercepting 15 Hurricanes that had tried to attack the bombers after the latter had hit their target. The unit claimed eight victories for the loss of a single Ki-43, with future aces Lts Shogo Takeuchi being credited with three kills and Yohei Hinoki two. No 258 Sqn had actually lost four aircraft to enemy action.

Both the 59th and 64th Sentais were awarded a handful of kills during the final death throes by the RAF in defence of Singapore, prior to moving to Kluang, in southern Malaya, on 6 February in preparation for operations over the Sumatran oilfields at Palembang. The 64th claimed the last Ki-43 kill over Singapore three days later when a No 232 Sqn Hurricane was shot down. The island finally fell to Japanese troops on 15 February.

By then both Ki-43 sentais had seen considerable action over Palembang, their pilots achieving air superiority over Sumatra during a series of bitter clashes with Allied fighters on 7 and 8 February that saw the 59th claim 16 victories and the 64th seven.

JAAF fighters had first been seen over Sumatra on 28 December 1941, when Ki-43s from the 59th Sentai had escorted Ki-48s sent to attack the airfield at Medan. Further long-range missions were flown on 16 and 17 January 1942, again involving the 59th Sentai. The JAAF returned in strength on 6 February, when no fewer than 32 Ki-43s from both sentais

Lt Shogo Takeuchi was one of the 64th Sentai's best pilots (he claimed three Hurricanes destroyed on 31 January 1942) prior to being transferred to the 68th Sentai in April 1942. Takeuchi would become an ace while flying the Ki-61 in New Guinea (*64th Sentai Association*)

15

CHAPTER ONE

escorted bombers sent to attack 50+ Allied aircraft spotted on the ground at Palembang's P1 airfield.

The first Sumatra-based aircraft to fall to the JAAF fighters were two Blenheim IVs from No 211 Sqn that were escorting a convoy bound for Singapore. One of the bombers was credited to future 14-kill ace Sgt Maj Hiroshi Onozaki of the 59th Sentai. The latter unit then pressed on to Palembang, where it engaged Hurricanes from Nos 232 and 258 Sqns. The Japanese pilots claimed five fighters shot down, with a further four aircraft destroyed on the ground.

P1 was attacked again the following day, with the Ki-43s bouncing the Hurricanes of No 258 Sqn just as they took off. Amongst the aces credited with victories were Sgt Maj Onozaki from the 59th and Lt Hinoki and Sgt Maj Yasuda of the 64th. Overall, ten RAF fighters and one Hudson were claimed to have been downed for the loss of a single Ki-43.

Two Hurricanes from No 232 Sqn were downed on 8 February, with single victories for both sentais. Ace Flt Lt Edwin Taylor and Sgt Sam Hackforth, who had four victories to his name, had both perished after losing turning fights with larger numbers of Ki-43s at low-level.

Five days later, seven replacement Hurricanes that had just reached Palembang from Tjililitan were bounced by fighters from the 59th Sentai and three were shot down. Two Ki-43s were lost in return, however.

On 14 February both sentais escorted 34 Ki-56s and Ki-57s carrying 460 paratroopers that were duly dropped in the Palembang area. A handful of Hurricanes were shot down as the Ki-43s kept RAF fighters away from both the vulnerable transports and wave after wave of JAAF bombers. The Japanese Army launched a successful seaborne assault on Sumatra early the following morning, and the Allied defence of the Dutch East Indies was doomed from that point on.

Within four days of the invasion commencing, the last Allied aircraft had fled Palembang and JAAF fighters (including 20 Ki-43s from the 64th Sentai) had occupied P1 airfield – it had been abandoned by the RAF just hours earlier. Shortly thereafter, all available Ki-43s were flown here from Malaya, allowing both sentais to seek out the enemy over western Java. They enjoyed their first success flying from P1 on the morning of 19 February, when pilots from both sentais claimed eight 'Curtiss Hawks' destroyed. They had in fact shot down three Dutch Buffaloes from 1- and 2-VlG-V, these aircraft having in turn attempted to engage Ki-48s sent to bomb Buitenzorg. The Buffaloes were the first of 33 victories credited to Ki-43 pilots between 19 and 25 February.

More success against Dutch fighters came the units' way on the afternoon of the 19th, when a dozen were intercepted during a bombing raid on Bandoeng. The Ki-43 pilots identified their opponents as Seversky P-43s! Although their identification skills were poor, their airmanship was not, and seven were claimed destroyed. As the sentais headed back to Palembang, they encountered a pair of USAAC B-17Es and shot one of them down. Its demise was credited to 59th Sentai ace WO Takeomi Hayashi, although fellow ace Sgt Maj Akeshi Yokoi of the 64th Sentai fell victim to defensive fire from one of the American bombers. He was duly rescued by an IJN floatplane. Yokoi and aces Capt Katsumi Anma and Sgt Yoshito Yasuda were amongst the pilots from the 64th to have downed Buffaloes earlier in this mission.

16

The next big action for both sentais was on 24 February, when JAAF pilots fought with seven Hurricanes from No 242 and 605 Sqns and four Dutch Curtiss CW-21Bs of 2-VlG-IV. Five Allied fighters were claimed as having been shot down. More aircraft, including a Martin bomber, additional Hurricanes and two Dornier Do 24 flying-boats, fell to the Ki-43s during the course of the day as further sweeps were flown over western Java.

The 59th Sentai claimed four more Hurricane kills on the 25th, thus raising the overall number of aircraft destroyed either in the air or on the ground by the JAAF's 3rd Flying Battalion to 86 in one week. Just three Ki-43s had been lost in action during the same period.

On 2 March Kalidjati airfield on Java was occupied by elements of the 59th Sentai as they returned from a bomber escort mission to Bandoeng. Several Dutch Martin bombers were subsequently destroyed by this unit as the Allies tried to render Kalidjati inoperable.

The 64th Sentai almost lost its CO on 3 March when Maj Kato's Ki-43 was shot up in error by A6M2s from the 3rd Kokutai. The ace was forced to crash-land at Kalidjati.

Several more British and Dutch fighters were downed over the next five days until, on 8 March, there were no airworthy enemy aircraft left in the East Indies. That same day Allied forces surrendered. The 64th Sentai would subsequently move to the Burma front in May 1942, having first made good its losses in men and materiel (the unit had had 13 pilots killed in three months of combat). The 59th, which boasted the leading Ki-43 ace of this period in Sgt Maj Hiroshi Onozaki with ten victories, would remain in the East Indies until late 1943.

Overall, both sentais had lost 73 fighters between them to all causes during this opening phase of the conflict in Asia, and by the end of the campaign in the East Indies, the 64th Sentai could muster just 15 operational Ki-43s. Nevertheless, the first stage of the Greater East Asian War had gone to plan, and the Nakajima fighter had played a key part in the success enjoyed by the JAAF.

Pilots of the 59th Sentai's 2nd Chutai relax between missions at Bandoeng airfield, in Java, in March 1942 *(Yasuho Izawa)*

The 64th Sentai captured three RAF Hurricane IIs at Palembang following the Allied evacuation of the East Indies, and at one time Lt Col Kato intended to use them in a surprise attack on their former owners. However, one Hurricane was lost in an accident that killed its pilot, Lt A Kikuchi, and another was burned out on the ground at Chiang Mai, in Thailand, on 24 March 1942. The third machine, seen in the background in this photograph, lasted long enough to be adorned with the sentai's arrow insignia. Indeed, the Hawker fighter even accompanied the 64th's 15 Ki-43s and two Ki-27s to Burma when the unit was posted to this theatre in May 1942 (*64th Sentai Association*)

COMBAT OVER BURMA

It was a JAAF headquarters public relations officer by the name of Maj Masaru Nishihara who bestowed the name Hayabusa (Peregrine Falcon) on the Ki-43 Type 1 Army fighter. It was a piece of wartime propaganda, and the name did not appear in Japanese newspaper reports until 8 March 1942 – well after the first stage of the Greater East Asian War had come to a successful end. The Allies had also given the Nakajima fighter the code name 'Oscar' by then too.

In contrast, the IJN's A6M Zero-Sen was never known by any other name (although the Allies referred to it as the 'Zeke'), and the Hayabusa became the more famous of the two fighters with the wartime Japanese public. Paradoxically, six decades later, the Zero-Sen is now far better known in Japan than the Ki-43. The author speculates that this is due to Western influences, as during the war, Allied combat reports classified most Japanese single-engined fighters as 'Zeros'. Afterwards, much of the available literature was of Western origin, and it concentrated on the successes achieved by the IJN fighter. Yet half the kills scored by Japanese fighter pilots in World War 2 were claimed by those flying Hayabusas.

And just as the Ki-43 had dominated the skies over Malaya, Singapore and the East Indies, it would enjoy success over Burma as Japan turned its attentions westward. The 64th Sentai had initially seen action over Rangoon during the large scale bombing raid of 25 December 1941. However, it had flown back to Malaya shortly after this operation, and would not return to the Burma front until 9 March 1942. The unit had been posted in to help the JAAF combat RAF Buffaloes and Hurricanes and AVG P-40s, all of which had enjoyed superiority over the agile but slow and lightly armed Ki-27s of the 50th and 77th Sentais.

The statistics for the Burma front from 11 December 1941 through to 7 March 1942 reveal just how much JAAF fighter units had struggled in this theatre. Between them, both sentais had lost 28 Ki-27s (as well as two Ki-43s on 25 December) and 26 pilots to Allied fighters. During the same period, the Allies had had seven Buffaloes, four Hurricanes and nine P-40s shot down, with 12 pilots killed.

On 9 March the 64th Sentai was transferred to Chieng Mai airfield, in Thailand, in preparation for operations over Burma. The unit arrived with 15 Ki-43s and two Ki-27s, as well as one captured Hurricane. It flew its first operational sorties a few days later, and on 21 March the sentai claimed its first kills since returning to Burma. Some 31 Ki-27s and 14 Ki-43s had escorted 52 Ki-21s sent to bomb the Allied airfield at Magwe, and they engaged a handful of AVG P-40Bs that went after the bombers. The JAAF pilots claimed eight fighters shot down for the loss of four of their own (at least one of which was a Ki-43). The 64th returned to Magwe the following day too.

The sentai escorted Ki-21s sent to bomb Akyab airfield on the 23rd, with a single Hurricane from No 136 Sqn being downed. The following morning it was the 64th Sentai's turn to be caught on the ground when six AVG P-40s strafed Chieng Mai. Three Ki-43s were destroyed and ten more damaged beyond repair. Two P-40s were downed by flak in return.

Despite the devastating losses on the morning of the 24th, the 64th still managed to sortie 11 fighters that afternoon as escorts for Ki-21s sent to attack Akyab once again. Three Hurricanes from No 136 Sqn were downed for the loss of a single Hayabusa. The sentai returned to Akyab three days later, downing another Hurricane and destroying seven more on the ground. The airfield had been abandoned by the Allies by dusk.

There followed a lull in the aerial action as the RAF tried to re-establish its Burma Wing at Lashio, near the Chinese border. The AVG had also pulled back to nearby Loiwing, and it was here that the 64th Sentai next saw action on a large scale on 8 April.

A Ki-46 reconnaissance aircraft had discovered that the Allies had retreated to the airfield 24 hours earlier, so Lt Col Tateo Kato (promoted on 19 February) decided to launch an audacious attack. His unit had seen three of its more experienced pilots posted back to Japan on 6 April, so three of the eight Ki-43s Kato led on the raid were flown by individuals lacking in combat experience. The Allies were warned by radar of the approaching Japanese formation, which was detected flying at 19,500 ft. Four Hurricanes and nine new P-40Es were immediately scrambled, and they were waiting for the 'Oscars' at 21,500 ft when they neared Loiwing.

The Japanese fighters were bounced as they commenced their first strafing pass. Keen to cause as much destruction as possible on the ground, Kato had decided against leaving two Ki-43s at altitude providing the attackers with top cover. 'It was carelessness', 64th Sentai ace Sgt Maj Yoshito Yasuda told the author. 'We had never suffered any surprise attacks in Malaya because we always made sure that we had top cover before we strafed targets on the ground'. The result was that Allied fighter pilots were able to claim 12 'Zeros' without loss to themselves. The 64th Sentai had actually lost four Ki-43s and their pilots, one of whom was 3rd Chutai leader (and 12-victory ace) Capt Katsumi Anma.

Kato then planned a surprise pre-dawn attack on Loiwing for 10 April. His pilots thought such a raid impossible because of the difficulty of navigating through a high mountain range in the dark. However, Kato was a highly skilled navigator, and he duly led four of his Ki-43s in an attack on Allied fighters as they sat on the ground at the base. The Japanese pilots failed to set fire to their targets though, as the fuel had been drained from the Allied aircraft as a precaution. 'I repeatedly strafed them but none would burn', Lt Yohei Hinoki later wrote.

Once back at base, Kato ordered another attack. His men were tired after four hours in the air, but nine Ki-43s led by the sentai CO appeared over Loiwing at 1705 hrs (Tokyo time). Their approach had again been detected by radar, and four AVG P-40Es were waiting for them at 24,000 ft. Four RAF Hurricanes from No 17 Sqn were also airborne. Sgt Maj Yoshito Yasuda was a participant in this mission;

'I was Lt Takeshi Endo's wingman. He spotted two fighters climbing at 19,500 ft over Loiwing, waggled his wings as a "tally ho" signal to Lt Col Kato, and gave chase.'

64th Sentai NCO ace Sgt Maj Yoshito Yasuda (centre) survived the war with ten victories to his name. The majority of his kills took the form of heavy bombers that were attempting to attack Rangoon. Hit by defensive fire whilst attacking a B-24 in late 1942, Yasuda was forced to bale out of his blazing fighter with serious burns. Hospitalised for several months, he was eventually sent back to Japan in July 1943 and subsequently served as an instructor at the Kumagaya Flying School. Promoted to warrant officer, he was posted to the 246th Sentai in April 1945 and flew in defence of the home islands. Flying Ki-84s, Yasuda claimed his final victory (a P-51) on 14 August 1945 – just 24 hours prior to the Japanese surrender (*Yoshito Yasuda*)

The formation led by Lt Hinoki followed, and its pilots soon spotted four Hurricanes flying in pairs, one above the other. One pair challenged Hinoki, while the other rushed at Endo. Kato wrongly assumed that the Hurricanes represented the total Allied fighter strength in the area, since he had over-estimated the effects of the morning's strafing attack. The nine Ki-43s chasing the Hurricanes were then jumped by four P-40Es.

Reacting quickly, Hinoki fired at two Warhawks attacking Endo's formation, and then went after the remaining pair. After one firing pass, he turned again to latch onto a diving P-40. His wingman, Sgt Maj Misago, lost him in the clouds, and when he found him again he saw that Hinoki had been hit and his fighter was trailing smoke. Misago drove two P-40s off his leader's tail, but moments later AVG pilot Flt Ldr Bob Brouk jumped him out of the sun and shot him down over the airfield.

Despite suffering from serious wounds, Hinoki somehow managed to limp home, where his groundcrew counted 21 bullet holes in his Ki-43. This was his first miracle escape.

Elsewhere during this fierce running battle, Sgt Maj Yoshito Yasuda had become separated from his flight leader, Lt Endo. He attacked an Allied in-line engined fighter and saw it crash into a hillside. Yasuda then ran out of ammunition. He assumed his victim had been a P-40, but years later learned that it was actually an RAF Hurricane. He then saw a pair of P-40s off to the west, but did not pay much attention to them.

They were the aircraft of Flt Ldrs Robert Hedman and Charles Older, who both turned to pursue Yasuda. They were closing from behind, firing as they did so, but when Yasuda saw the tracers streaking past him, and felt his Ki-43 shudder, he thought that his guns had discharged accidentally. Glancing over his shoulder, he realised that he had two P-40s just 650 yards behind him. Older was surprised when Yasuda pulled up into a loop, and he overshot the nimble Ki-43. Hedman stuck to Yasuda's tail, however, bearing down on him. Yasuda again manoeuvred violently. 'I opened the canopy for better visibility, but the blast of air dried out my throat – I'll never forget that pain', he told the author.

The combatants had lost altitude during 30 minutes of violent manoeuvring. In the end, Hedman and Older thought that they had scored a kill when they saw the hard-hit Ki-43 limp off towards a mountain range trailing thick black smoke. Yasuda recalled, 'After I landed and had a look at my aeroplane, I found no fewer than 17 bullet holes in it. We had lost six Ki-43s and pilots in two days of fighting. It was the biggest defeat that the 64th Sentai experienced throughout the war'. These casualties took the sentai's overall pilot losses since 7 December 1941 to 30, eight of whom had been killed in just three clashes with the AVG.

In order to make good the loss of Capt Anma, the 64th Sentai's 3rd Chutai welcomed Capt Yasuhiko Kuroe from the 47th Independent Chutai on 24 April. Kuroe, who had claimed two kills with the 59th Sentai during the Nomonhan Incident and three with the 47th over Singapore and Malaya in pre-production Ki-44 Shoki fighters, would ultimately down 24 Allied aircraft with the Ki-43.

Two more 'Oscars' fell to the AVG on 28 April when the sentai escorted Ki-21s sent to attack Loiwing. One pilot was killed and the second returned to base on foot. Despite these reversals in the air, the Japanese Army was steadily advancing northward, forcing the Allies to abandon Lashio and Loiwing on 30 April. The AVG had fled to bases in 'free China', and the JAAF bombed one such site at Paoshan on 4 May. A single P-40E was downed by the 64th, led by Capt Kuroe, although not before its pilot had destroyed a Ki-21.

On 12 May the sentai began sending Ki-43s from its new base at Toungoo, in southeastern Burma, to Akyab, on the Burmese west coast. Two-thirds of the crews transferred to the latter base quickly came down with dengue fever, including Capt Kuroe. 'I was ashamed with myself, being in such bad shape and causing the unit so much trouble so soon after getting the job', he later recalled. Kuroe was visited in hospital by Lt Col Kato, who told him that his illness proved that he 'was human too'.

Despite disease being rife, the detachment claimed its first kill on 17 May when future ace Lt Saburo Nakamura downed a No 62 Sqn Hudson. A witness to this action was Lt Ichiro Niimi. Checking his wristwatch as he and Endo sat on a bench in the pilots' ready hut at Akyab airfield, he commented 'The sentai commander will be here soon'. They had sighted a small dot in the southern sky. Both officers stood up and strode out to meet Lt Col Kato. But something about the sound of the approaching aircraft alerted Niimi. 'Air raid!' he shouted, and dived into a trench.

The lone Hudson had arrived to discover that Akyab's anti-aircraft defence consisted of just two machine guns. Its pilot made the most of his opportunity to attack a valuable target, before being shot down by Kato's wingman, Lt Nakamura. It was his first kill, and the groundcrew welcomed him with cheers when he climbed out of his Ki-43.

Sgt Maj Yasuda claimed another No 62 Sqn Hudson on 21 May when he chased it to within 20 miles of Chittagong. The airfield at this location had also been strafed that same day by eight Ki-43s led by Lt Col Kato. Although no RAF aircraft were encountered, during the return flight the 'Oscar' of nine-kill ace and 1st Chutai top scorer WO Takeshi Shimizu burst into flames and he baled out over Allied territory.

Kato had planned to leave Akyab after returning from Chittagong, but he decided to remain at the base an extra night and hope for news of Shimizu's return – he had, however, been taken prisoner. That evening, Kato talked far into the night with his officers about a variety of subjects, such as a trip to Europe in July 1939 when he had visited the Luftwaffe and flown a Bf 109. Such informality was unusual for the veteran sentai commander, who, at 38, was technically too old to be leading a frontline fighter unit, yet had been flying two or three sorties per day since the war had started.

On the morning of 22 May, Kato sent for Yasuda, praised him for his victory, and took a photograph of his subordinate with his Leica camera. Minutes later they were interrupted by a lone No 60 Sqn Blenheim IV, which attacked

On 17 May 1942, Lt Saburo Nakamura of the 64th Sentai shot down a Hudson of No 62 Sqn shortly after it had attacked Akyab airfield. This victory was to be the first of 20 officially credited to Nakamura over the next two-and-a-half years. He had previously served with the 1st Sentai in Manchuria prior to joining the 64th in April 1942 (Yasuho Izawa)

This grainy photograph was the last one to be taken of Lt Col Tateo Kato, the 64th Sentai CO sitting on a stool examining a map with a fellow pilot at Akyab airfield. He was shot down and killed on 22 May 1942 by the turret gunner of a No 60 Sqn Blenheim IV (*64th Sentai Association*)

Pilots of the 64th Sentai got to experience the flying characteristics of the P-40E when this airworthy example was put through its paces at Mingaladon. It had been captured intact when the AVG abandoned its Burmese bases in the spring of 1942. Lt Saburo Nakamura was just one of a handful of aces that got to fly the Curtiss fighter, noting in his diary that he had performed combat manoeuvres with the aircraft on 12 July 1942 (*64th Sentai Association*)

Akyab. Kato immediately scrambled with four other Ki-43s and gave chase as the bomber raced back over the Bay of Bengal at low-level. The Blenheim's turret gunner, Flt Sgt 'Jock' McLuckie, proved to be an outstanding shot, as he quickly wounded Yasuda and damaged Capt Masuzo Otani's fighter.

Kato then dived at the Blenheim, and McLuckie raked the underside of the Ki-43 as its pilot pulled up in order to avoid hitting the sea. The fighter began to burn, then 'wobbled' and rolled over into the sea. Having realised that he could not nurse his fighter home, Kato had taken his own life – he had often advised his pilots to follow a similar course of action in the circumstances.

On landing back at Akyab, the shocked Yasuda damaged his fighter when he ran into a ditch alongside the runway. As Capt Kuroe was about to reprimand him, Yasuda blurted out, 'The sentai commander has been killed!' Kato was posthumously promoted two ranks to major general. The loss of the JAAF's first great fighter ace, whose score then stood at 18 (ten in China), had a terrible effect on the morale of the 64th Sentai.

Yasuda took the opportunity to avenge his CO on 4 June when, flying as wingman to Lt Takemura, he caught a B-17E of the 436th BS over Rangoon and made four firing passes at it. The bomber caught fire but Yasuda lost it in cloud. The damaged aircraft was later attacked by three Ki-27s of the 77th Sentai over Magwe, and it belly-landed in a rice paddy. The B-17 was the JAAF's first victory over a heavy bomber in Burma.

Several days later, the onset of the monsoon season effectively ended the first campaign in Burma. Between March and June 1942, the 64th Sentai had lost 11 Ki-43s and ten pilots in aerial combat. Apart from the Blenheim that had accounted for Lt Col Kato, AVG P-40s were responsible for all losses. The aerial victory claims made by the 'Oscar' pilots during this period matched reported Allied losses – one P-40, six Hurricanes, two Hudsons, one Blenheim and the B-17E.

Monsoon rains prevented further operations being conducted either in the air or on the ground until early September. The JAAF used the break to reorganise its forces in preparation for the re-commencement of 'shooting season' come the autumn, with both Ki-27 sentais being replaced in Burma by the Ki-43-Ib-equipped 11th and 50th Sentais.

The latter unit, posted in from Singapore, and led by Maj Tadashi Ishikawa, arrived at Mingaladon in early September. Many of the 50th Sentai pilots had previously seen combat flying Ki-27s in the Philippines and Burma.

The unit's first combat mission with the Hayabusa came on the morning of 9 September, when the 2nd Chutai provided fighter cover for a convoy of vessels heading for Akyab. The Ki-43s flew from Mingaladon to Magwe airfield, in central Burma, and as the convoy entered Akyab port nine Blenheim IVs from Nos 60 and 113 Sqns attempted to attack the ships. Japanese newspapers reported at the time;

'It was a rainy day and the overcast was down to 1000 ft. The six young warriors of the Ishikawa Sentai, led by Capt Masao Miyamaru, spotted 12 Blenheims coming from the west at 300 ft. The Ki-43s of the 50th Sentai's 2nd Chutai intercepted them. Lt Akira Takano aimed at the lead bomber, controlling his impatience. Lt Murayama, Sgt Majs Oyagawa and Uguchi, and Sgt Miyake followed him from the clouds. The bombers dropped their bombs and spread out, at which point they were attacked. Takano made a head-on attack on the leading bomber and shot it down. Murayama chased another bomber at very low altitude. He caught it and fired a long burst at it. The bomber crashed into the sea. Despite fierce defensive fire, Miyake rushed at a further bomber and shot it down in a head-on pass. The groundcrew later found 16 bullet holes in his Ki-43.

'Two hours later, two Hudson formations of three aircraft appeared, in spite of the bitter experience suffered by their comrades earlier in the day. Capt Miyamaru spotted them first and dived at a bomber like a swallow. His first burst silenced the turret gunner. He chased the Hudson and shot it down into the sea. Capt Miyamaru then turned and caught another. It too belched flames and crashed.'

The 50th Sentai received 45 new Ki-43-Is at Tokorozawa, near Tokyo, on 8 June 1942. Seen here still undergoing their conversion training in Japan, these pilots include unit CO Maj Tadashi Ishikawa (farthest from the camera in flying helmet) and 2nd Chutai leader and future ace Capt Masao Miyamaru (front row, third from right). Note the sentai's recently applied lightning bolt insignia on the tails of the factory-fresh Ki-43-Is sat on the Tokorozawa flightline (*Shunkichi Kikuchi*)

Briefing over, 50th Sentai pilots practise formation flying over Tokorozawa airfield in June 1942 (*Shunkichi Kikuchi*)

The Blenheims had completed their task before being jumped by the Ki-43s, and the 2019-ton cargo vessel *Niyou-maru* was severely damaged. In all, the 50th Sentai claimed to have shot down five bombers – No 113 Sqn lost two and No 60 Sqn one. Another Blenheim was shot up so badly that it had to return on one engine, while a No 62 Sqn Hudson failed to make it back to base and another was badly damaged.

Nos 60 and 113 Sqns could hardly have chosen a worse time to raid Akyab. The 2nd Chutai had provided three Ki-43s for continuous top cover of the port since dawn, and the Blenheims arrived at changeover time, and were consequently intercepted by six 'Oscars'. Capt Masao Miyamaru would be credited with eight kills prior to his death in 1944.

The 50th's 1st and 2nd Chutais claimed six more Blenheims out of a force of 18 that attacked another Akyab convoy on 14 October.

The 64th Sentai, now led by Maj Masami Yagi, had also been busy during the monsoon season, as it had re-equipped with 30 of the latest Ki-43 model II-Hei (C)s fitted with twin 12.7 mm guns. These aircraft had been flown to the sentai's base at Mingaladon from Java, where pilots had received special training in attacking four-engined heavy bombers using an airworthy B-17E captured in the East Indies. Capt Kuroe had flown as a passenger in the bomber's nose to watch his men making their head-on passes – some of the latter had been so close that he instinctively flinched. Following their rigorous training regime in the East Indies, Kuroe was satisfied that morale was high.

The 11th Sentai, which had seen much action over Malaya, the East Indies and Burma in Ki-27s, swapped its 'Nates' for Ki-43-Is in Japan in July 1942 and returned to Mingaladon three months later. It would not remain in-theatre for long, however, as it was sent to Rabaul West to help bolster the JAAF's fighter force in New Guinea in December 1942.

The 1st Sentai had also exchanged its Ki-27s for Ki-43-Is at the Akeno Fighter School, in Japan, during the monsoon season, this unit being sent to Tourane, in French Indochina, upon its return to the frontline in October 1942. Like the 11th Sentai, the 1st would also be posted to New Guinea two months later.

A series of airfield strafing attacks were flown by all four Ki-43 sentais from 22 October, with Chittagong being an early target. On the 25th the JAAF launched major strikes on Allied airfields at Dinjan and Chabua, in Assam. The attacks were mounted by 27 Ki-21s of the 14th Sentai, escorted by 36 Ki-43s from the 64th Sentai, and by 27 Ki-48s of the 8th Sentai, escorted by 45 Ki-43s from the 50th Sentai.

Two P-40Es of the USAAF's 51st FG were preparing to take off on an armed reconnaissance mission when the raiders appeared over Dinjan without warning. Six P-40s attempted to scramble, and Capt Kuroe spotted them and dived to attack, but his speed was too high. He barely had time to fire at a P-40

64th Sentai pilots look over an airworthy B-17E that was captured in Java in March 1942. The unit flew a series of training sorties against this aircraft over Singapore on 4 October 1942 as pilots honed the tactics that would be employed against Allied heavy bombers sent to attack Rangoon later that year (*64th Sentai Association*)

when he flew over five others. Kuroe then targeted a sixth Warhawk, whose pilot was still retracting his landing gear. His wingman, Sgt Maj Yasuda, also fired at it, and the P-40 crash-landed amongst nearby trees.

Over Chabua, meanwhile, two more P-40Es from the 51st FG had attacked Lt Fukui, who was leading the right-hand flight of the 50th Sentai's 3rd Chutai. Sgt Satoshi Anabuki, who would become the most successful Ki-43 ace, spotted the P-40s above and behind Fukui, and fired a short burst ahead of his leader as a warning. The lead P-40 failed to catch Fukui and his wingman, while Anabuki managed to avoid a second fighter that overshot him. He then became involved in a dogfight that resulted in the future JAAF ace shooting the P-40 down into a rice paddy. It was the first victory that Anabuki had scored in his new Ki-43, christened *Fubuki Snowstorm*. His previous kills had been claimed with the Ki-27.

Sgt Satoshi Anabuki of the 50th Sentai/3rd Chutai was the JAAF's top ace with 39 aerial victories to his credit. Some 30 of these kills came while flying the Ki-43 in Burma between June 1942 and October 1943 (*Yasuho Izawa*)

On 10 November it was the 64th Sentai's turn to tangle with RAF bombers when five Ki-43s of the 1st Chutai, led by Capt Haruyasu Maruo, intercepted eight Blenheims of Nos 60 and 113 Sqns, and their escort of eight No 155 Sqn Mohawk IVs, whilst providing top cover for an Akyab-bound troop transport vessel. Three of the Ki-43 NCO pilots were about to participate in their first aerial combat.

Capt Maruo ordered 3rd Chutai leader Capt Kuroe to take on the fighters while he headed for the bombers. Lt Saburo Nakamura reached the Blenheims first, but was attacked by four Mohawk IVs. Moments later Maruo was shot down and killed from behind – his tail had been left unprotected when he and his NCO wingman became separated during the opening stages of the dogfight. The RAF lost two Mohawk IVs.

By the time Kuroe arrived on the scene the air battle was over. He saw future 20-victory ace Lt Nakamura circling over a black patch of oil on the sea, the latter having taken on four Mohawk IVs single-handedly and claimed two destroyed for his second and third kills. His wingman, novice Sgt Kuribayashi, had quickly lost sight of his leader in the engagement. Despite the loss of two Mohawk IVs, both JAAF and RAF pilots felt that the Curtiss fighter was almost as manoeuvrable as the Ki-43.

Several hours later, six Ki-43s of the 64th Sentai, led by Lt Shunji Takahashi, provided top cover for another ship heading for Akyab. The vessel was attacked by 11 Blenheim IVs, escorted by four Mohawk IVs. Capt Kuroe overheard Takahashi on his radio excitedly ordering his wingmen to attack the bombers spotted by WO Yamada. Young and impetuous Takahashi flew directly at the Blenheims, but highly-experienced ace Sgt Maj Shokichi Omori spotted the Mohawk IVs above the bombers and climbed up towards them on his own.

Three more Ki-43s then joined the battle, one of which collided with a Mohawk IV and was lost – thanks to the tough construction of the Curtiss fighter, it survived the incident and limped home. Two Blenheims had been downed by the 64th, however, and a third bomber destroyed by flak.

Capt Haruyasu Maruo arrived from Japan to assume leadership of the 64th Sentai's 1st Chutai in January 1942 following the death of Capt Saburo Takahashi in action over Malaya in late December 1941. Maruo was in turn killed on 10 November 1942 after his tail was left exposed to attack by RAF Mohawk IVs during a dogfight near Akyab (*64th Sentai Association*)

Maj Tadashi Ishikawa (centre, with glasses) led the 50th Sentai from March 1942 through to August 1943, claiming several kills during this period (*Yasuho Izawa*)

A veteran of the Nomonhan Incident, 50th Sentai eight-victory ace 2Lt Teizo Kanamaru was killed (along with his groundcrew) at Magwe North airfield by bombs dropped by an RAF Blenheim shortly before dawn on 24 December 1942. His comrades (including Sgt Anabuki) avenged his death later that same day when his chutai claimed to have shot down three Hurricanes (*Yasuho Izawa*)

The next victory credited to the Ki-43 came on the night of 26 November, when Capt Kuroe and Sgt Maj Yasuda used all their combat experience to destroy a B-24 over Rangoon. This victory gave the JAAF its first nocturnal success over the Burmese capital.

Chittagong was again singled out for attention by the JAAF on 5 December, when the 50th and 64th Sentais sortied aircraft to escort 24 heavy bombers sent to attack the city. The 64th claimed a single victory when 2nd Chutai leader Capt Masuzo Ohtani shot down a Mohawk IV, but moments later he in turn fell victim to a second Curtiss fighter.

Five days later, Chittagong was again attacked by 21 Ki-48s of the 8th Sentai, escorted by 24 Ki-43s from the 50th and 12 from the 64th Sentais. Hurricanes from Nos 135 and 136 Sqns attempted to intercept the bombers, but they were jumped from above by the escorts. Capt Kuroe saw fighters from the 50th Sentai send two No 135 Sqn Hurricanes crashing into the sea, one of whom had fallen victim to unit CO Maj Tadashi Ishikawa and the other to future nine-kill ace Lt Shigeru Nakazaki.

The 50th Sentai was in action again over Chittagong on 15 December, and its pilots (including Sgt Anabuki) claimed six Hurricanes destroyed for the loss of a single Ki-43. The following day, the 64th Sentai was posted back to Tachikawa, near Tokyo, to re-equip with Ki-43-IIs. The 50th Sentai's 20 Ki-43-Ibs would now provide the only JAAF fighter presence on the Burma front until February 1943.

16 December also saw the 50th Sentai scoring more kills when it escorted 20 Ki-51s that had been sent to attack Feni airfield. Three Hurricanes from Nos 607 and 615 Sqns and a Hudson from No 194 Sqn were shot down for the loss of a single Ki-43, whose pilot was captured.

In response to the airfield raids in December, the RAF targeted JAAF bases at Magwe and Akyab in the lead up to Christmas. The former was hit first on the 20th, when three Ki-43s engaged 14 Blenheims and 12 Hurricanes. Despite his aircraft being struck by shrapnel from exploding ordnance as he hastily took off, Lt Nakazaki quickly turned the tables and claimed two Hurricanes destroyed, while fellow ace Sgt Anabuki downed a Hurricane and a Blenheim. Both pilots also claimed a Hurricane apiece two days later during an escort mission to Feni.

Shortly before dawn on Christmas Eve, the RAF attacked Magwe North airfield and caught two night-alert 50th Sentai Ki-43s parked out in the open. Their bombs killed eight-victory ace 2Lt Teizo Kanamaru and his groundcrew, who were attempting to start the engine of his fighter when it suffered a direct hit. A second Ki-43 was also set on fire, but Sgt Satoshi Anabuki was able to get airborne and claim a Blenheim shot down – all the RAF bombers made it home safely, however.

Seven Hurricanes returned to Magwe that afternoon, four of which were Mk IICs of No 615 Sqn equipped with a quartet of 20 mm cannon. The Magwe air defence had been reinforced by four more Ki-43s following the Blenheim raid, and the RAF machines arrived just as six Japanese fighters started to take off. Four No 607 Sqn Hurricanes dived to strafe the defending anti-aircraft guns, while a hail of 20 mm shells from the No 615 Sqn aircraft caught the final pair of 'Oscars' to depart Magwe. The aircraft of 3rd Chutai leader Lt Nakazaki and Sgt Maj Sou were seen to be trailing white smoke as they went after the Hurricanes.

Future ace Anabuki quickly shot down the Hurricane IIC of Sgt E Kostromin, whilst the No 607 Sqn Hurricane of Flg Off C D Fergusson was also brought down. It was not until after the battle that Anabuki noticed that he had forgotten to retract his undercarriage! No Ki-43s were lost, despite Lt Nakazaki having had a smoking engine throughout the engagement – he claimed two Hurricanes destroyed. However, Sgt Maj Sou, whose fighter had also been hit, was affected by petrol fumes seeping into his cockpit, and as he landed, his Ki-43 overran the runway and ended up in the trees. Sou emerged from the wreckage unhurt.

This proved to be the last action of note involving Ki-43s until mid-January, when the JAAF was thrown back into the fight in earnest in response to the Allied offensive down the Mayu Peninsula. Nakazaki and Anabuki each claimed a Hurricane destroyed north of Akyab on the 14th, and two days later the 50th Sentai took part in an attack on Kunming Station south airfield in China. Three P-40s were claimed for the loss of a single Ki-43. On the 18th the 'Oscar' pilots escorted bombers sent to attack Feni, and they were credited with destroying four Hurricanes.

On 23 January, 16 Ki-43s rendezvoused with 17 Ki-21s from the 98th Sentai and headed for Chittagong. Two 'Oscars' from the 3rd Chutai had to return because of mechanical trouble before they reached the target, and the remaining fighters were intercepted by eight Hurricanes from No 136 Sqn and three from No 135 Sqn. Lt Nakazaki, who was flying Sgt Anabuki's Ki-43 on this occasion, formed the formation's rear guard with his 3rd Chutai, and it was he and his two wingmen that bore the brunt of the attack launched by the 12 Hurricanes.

Nakazaki latched onto the tail of a Hurricane from No 136 Sqn, while another RAF fighter got in behind the JAAF ace and opened fire. His Ki-43 was hit hard in the engine, and streaming fuel, Nakazaki headed away from the area with fellow ace Sgt Maj Noboru Mune as his escort. Realising that he would not make it back to Akyab, Nakazaki turned his aircraft around and headed for Allied territory. Spotting an enemy ship off the Arakan coast just as his engine stopped, Nakazaki crashed his Ki-43 into it and was killed. The 50th Sentai claimed three Hurricanes that day, although RAF losses amounted to just one fighter and its pilot.

The following day the 50th was credited with the destruction of two Wellingtons over Rangoon. On the 26th, 14 B-24s of the 7th BG appeared over the Burmese capital at 20,000 ft. Battling through accurate and intense flak, the US crews saw several formations of JAAF fighters flying parallel to them. Turning ahead of the bombers, they then commenced a series of head-on attacks. Six Ki-43s claimed four B-24s destroyed, but all the USAAF bombers returned to base with varying degrees of damage – all the Ki-43s were also damaged by defensive fire from the heavy bombers. Four pilots had expended all their ammunition, showing that the B-24 was a hard nut for the lightly armed Ki-43 to crack.

The 50th claimed two Hurricanes destroyed on 3 February, and the following day it withdrew to Singapore for re-equipment with Ki-43-IIs.

During its single-handed defence of Japanese-held Burma between December 1942 and February 1943, the 50th Sentai had claimed 40 aerial victories. But Allied records showed that only seven aircraft – five Hurricanes and two P-40s – had in fact been lost. Three sentai pilots had been killed during the same period.

50th Sentai/3rd Chutai leader, and nine-victory ace, Capt Shigeru Nakazaki dived his aircraft into an Allied hospital ship after it was badly damaged by a Hurricane from No 136 Sqn on 23 January 1943 (*Yasuho Izawa*)

The 50th was relieved in the frontline by the 64th Sentai, which returned to Toungoo with its Ki-43-IIs in early February. Not only was the newer aircraft 12 mph faster than the Ki-43-I, it also had the Type 1 gunsight. This was easier to use and caused less drag than the telescopic sight. The new aircraft also had a thicker 13 mm outer rubber coating for its fuel tanks to provide some protection against 0.5-in incendiary bullets.

However, early production Ki-43-IIs lacked armour protection for the pilot's back. The 13 mm back and 8 mm head armour arrived with aircraft number 5194 – the 194th Nakajima-built Ki-43 (number '5' signified the Nakajima factory). According to 64th Sentai/2nd Chutai engineer Lt Atushi Ueda, the first two Ki-43s featuring armour protection for the pilot were not delivered to the unit until 19 July 1943.

Despite this omission, the Ki-43-II was still ahead of the A6M Zero-sen in self-protection, as the IJN fighter was never fitted with rubber-coated fuel tanks or pilot armour. These improvements came at a price, for the extra weight associated with them made the Ki-43-II's rate of climb and turning ability inferior to that of the older model.

Just as important as the new features was the fighter's increased strength, and the greater confidence this gave its pilots. 'I felt that we could wreak havoc at will', Sgt Maj Yoshito Yasuda recalled. 'We were at last relieved of the fear of mid-air disintegration'. But Lt Ueda told the author that although there were no further accidents through wing failure, 'we found wrinkles on the wing surface of some Model IIs too'. A Nakajima engineer inspected the aircraft in Rangoon and installed springs over the control wires so as to reduce G-loads in turns. All Model IIs would be modified in Singapore during the 1943 monsoon season.

The 64th saw its first combat with the Ki-43-II on 12 February when four aircraft were bounced by two Mohawk IVs. Having escorted bombers out of the forward area, the 'Oscars' had returned to strafe the airstrip at Kyaktaw. The only casualty from this engagement was sentai CO Maj Masami Yagi, who was killed by a single bullet to the head. The following day Capt Kuroe led 12 Ki-43s on an escort mission for six light bombers sent to attack Donbaik. They encountered four Hurricanes from No 261 Sqn shortly after shepherding the bombers safely back south, and in the bitter dogfight that ensued, the unit lost 2nd Chutai leader Capt Jiro Seki and Cpl Umeda. Four Hurricanes were claimed in return, although only a single RAF fighter was actually downed.

Lt Nakamura and his wingman, Sgt Miyoshi Watanabe, had attacked a jinking Hurricane at low altitude, and it came down in the River Nuf. They shared the victory, which took Nakamura's tally to four and gave future eight-kill ace Watanabe his first success. Nakamura force-landed upon his return to Akyab due to battle damage. As he extricated himself from his fighter, he saw Watanabe engage two No 79 Sqn Hurricanes that had been strafing targets in the area. His wingman successfully attacked the fighter flown by Sgt R North, who crash-landed on a nearby beach.

New 64th Sentai CO Maj Takeyo Akera led 11 Ki-43s as escorts for three Ki-48s sent to bomb forward positions on 20 February. Eight 'Oscars' then strafed Maungdaw 1 advanced fighter base from the sea. Three Hurricanes from No 135 Sqn scrambled to intercept the attackers, and when they reached 14,500 ft, three Ki-43s jumped them. Akera's wingman, Sgt Hirano, set Plt Off C Fox's Hurricane on fire and the pilot baled out. WO A Campbell's fighter was also badly shot up but he was able to dive away, leaving Flt Lt G Booyson on his own.

Capt Kuroe, flying top cover, soon spotted the lone Hurricane in front of him and he dived on it, firing a burst from 325 yards. One of his wingmen, future ten-kill ace Sgt Maj Yoshito Yasuda, also fired at the Hurricane, which broke away to the left and dived for the ground. Another wingman, Sgt Maj Hosogaya, also fired at the diving Hurricane, which was then attacked once again by Kuroe. Like Fox's machine, Booyson's fighter plunged into the jungle after what had been a good example of formation combat by well disciplined Japanese pilots.

Maj Akera was not to command the 64th for long, however, as on the 25th he was shot down by P-40Es from the 51st FG whilst escorting bombers sent to attack targets in Assam. Capt Kuroe was made deputy CO at this time, and all the sentai's flight leaders were also promoted – Lt Takahashi became 1st Chutai deputy leader, Lt Nakamura 2nd Chutai deputy leader and Lt Tadashi Kurosawa 3rd Chutai deputy leader.

A single chutai from the 50th Sentai had also participated in this mission on 25 February. The unit had received 20 Model IIs on 10 February whilst in Surabaya, Java, and its pilots immediately started converting onto the new fighter. The first chutai to be declared operational returned to Meiktila, in Burma, on 20 February.

Eight days, later both the 50th and 64th Sentais put up a combined force of 20 Ki-43s against a raid by six Blenheims of No 60 Sqn, escorted by seven Hurricanes from No 136 Sqn. The JAAF fighters were led by Capt Kuroe, who spotted the aircraft attacking Japanese ground forces near Akyab. Ordering his eight Ki-43s to engage the Hurricanes, he fired a single burst that hit the radiator of Sgt D Barnett's fighter, forcing him to bale out, while Flt Sgt F Wilding belly-landed at Ramu airfield.

Kuroe then chased after two more Hurricanes, catching one at low altitude – Sgt P Kennedy parachuted to safety. Three fighters had been lost by No 136 Sqn in just a matter of minutes. Seven Hurricanes and a Blenheim were claimed in total, with Sgt Anabuki of the 50th Sentai being credited with the lone bomber (none were lost) and a fighter.

March 1943 was to see considerable action for both Ki-43 sentais, as the JAAF's 5th Air Division commenced an operation that was intended to secure air superiority over the Akyab area in support of a Japanese counterattack in the Mayu Peninsula. The first action came during a strafing attack on Feni on the 2nd conducted by aircraft from both units. The 50th claimed two Hurricanes shot down near the base and the 64th was credited with two more during the return flight.

The Japanese offensive was launched on 5 March, and that day the 64th fought two engagements with No 136 Sqn over Akyab. During the first of these, Capt Kuroe and his formation of five took on Nos 79 and 697 Sqns, which were escorting Blenheims sent to attack Yeganbyin. They claimed six fighters destroyed (only one was lost), with both Kuroe and future ten-kill ace Sgt Kosuke Tsubone being credited with victories. A single Ki-43 was downed in return. In the afternoon, the unit again fought No 135 Sqn, but this time four Ki-43s were destroyed.

Following a brief break in operations, the 64th Sentai appeared over the frontline once again on 14 March when deputy CO Capt Kuroe led 15 Ki-43s on a fighter sweep over Donbaik. They intercepted three

64th Sentai/2nd Chutai NCO aces Sgts Kosuke Tsubone (left) and Miyoshi Watanabe pose for the camera in Burma in early 1943. The former would claim ten aerial victories and survive the war, whilst the latter, who frequently broke formation and engaged in individual combat despite the JAAF believing in the importance of maintaining formation, scored eight victories in just three months prior to being killed on 29 May 1943 (*Yasuho Izawa*)

Blenheims of No 11 Sqn, escorted by ten No 135 Sqn Hurricanes, near Maungdaw. Kuroe fired a 200-round burst from behind at a Hurricane before making way for his wingman, Lt Ishii, who shot the fighter down during his very first combat. With the Hurricanes scattered, Sgt Miyoshi Watanabe broke up the bomber formation and downed a Blenheim.

The 64th was in action again the next day, when it provided 14 escorts for an identical number of Ki-48s from the 34th Sentai that were sent to bomb Rathedaung. En route, they encountered Hurricanes from Nos 136 and 607 Sqns as they shepherded 12 Blenheims sent to attack Japanese targets. A Hurricane gushed black smoke after being attacked by Kuroe, who continued to chase it, firing until it exploded. Flg Off F Pickard and Wt Off A Cruyenaere of No 136 Sqn were killed, while No 607 Sqn lost Flg Off W Gibbs and Plt Off L Main. WO D Blyth's Hurricane was also hit, and force-landed at Maungdaw 1. A Blenheim was also destroyed and two more so badly damaged that they crash-landed upon returning to base. All the Ki-43s got back safely.

Sgt Watanabe claimed two Hurricanes for his fourth and fifth kills, although the author has been unable to find any corroborating evidence. The 64th Sentai was credited with the destruction of eight Hurricanes in total, with Lt Nakamura reporting that his 2nd Chutai had accounted for four of them – none of the successful pilots were named, however.

The JAAF's strike on the 16th was uneventful, but on the 17th, whilst escorting bombers attacking Ramu airfield, the 64th Sentai shot down a No 79 Sqn Hurricane and damaged four more (two of which were written off) without loss. Three fighters were claimed by the sentai, with Capt Kuroe and Lt Takahashi being credited with two of them. The 64th was credited with two more victories on the 18th, having tangled with both Hurricanes from No 135 Sqn and Beaufighters from No 27 Sqn.

By mid March all three chutais within the 50th Sentai had arrived at Meiktila, and on the 24th the unit bounced nine USAAF B-25s. All were claimed to have been shot down for the loss of one Ki-43. The sentai also downed three Hurricanes on the 26th, and Lt Sanae Ishii of the 64th Sentai claimed the first Beaufighter to be acknowledged as lost by the RAF.

Although the 50th had got off to a great start with the Ki-43-II, all this was forgotten on 27 March when it failed to rendezvous with 25 Ki-48s heading for Cox's Bazaar. Making the most of the situation, Hurricanes from Nos 79 and 135 Sqns downed five bombers without loss.

Attempting to restore its reputation, the 50th claimed heavily over the next four days, with six Hurricanes being shot down on the 28th and 11 on the 30th – according to RAF records, only one Hurricane and one Mohawk were lost during this period.

The 50th would actually inflict significant losses on the RAF's fighter force on the last day of the month, however. Eight hand-picked combat veterans (all of whom would ultimately become 'Oscar' aces) from the sentai, led by their CO, Maj Tadashi Ishikawa, departed Meiktila soon after dawn and attacked the advanced Allied airfield at Pataga. Having made their strafing runs, the Ki-43 pilots climbed to 19,000 ft east of Buthidaung and formed up into a formation dubbed the 'beehive' by RAF pilots. Keen for a fight, the JAAF pilots moved steadily southward, enticing the ten Hurricane pilots from No 135 Sqn that had been scrambled to intercept them to head deeper into Japanese-held territory.

The 64th Sentai's Capt Hideo Miyabe arrived at Toungoo airfield to succeed 2nd Chutai deputy leader Lt Nakamura on 15 March 1943. Miyabe would eventually become the sentai's last commanding officer, and he had claimed ten aerial victories by war's end (*Yasuho Izawa*)

Using their superior height and speed, the 'Oscar' pilots bounced the RAF fighters as they climbed up through the heavy mist that blanketed the area. In the fierce dogfight that ensued, the 50th Sentai claimed to have shot eight Hurricanes down and probably destroyed six more – the Ki-43 pilots reported that they had engaged no fewer than 40 Hurricanes and P-40s! Three RAF fighters had actually been destroyed, with a fourth machine badly shot up. Future eight-kill ace Capt Masao Miyamaru claimed three, and his wingman, Sgt Yukio Shimokawa (who would eventually achieve a score of 16), was credited with downing two.

That same day, the 64th Sentai managed to shoot down a B-24 of the 9th BS, but return fire badly damaged the Ki-43 of new 2nd Chutai leader (and future ten-kill ace) Capt Hideo Miyabe and he was forced to make a crash-landing – his engine had been hit by the B-24's intense defensive fire. Picked up by a JAAF truck, Miyabe found a B-24 crewman surrounded by excited Burmese civilians upon his return to Magwe airfield. A Japanese groundcrew sergeant major confiscated the American's pistol and took him to Magwe with Miyabe.

The JAAF took another beating from the RAF on 1 April when three Ki-21s were shot down during a raid on Feni. Because so many of the 64th Sentai's Ki-43s had been damaged by the B-24s the day before, the unit could only put up ten fighters. A solitary Hurricane from No 615 Sqn was shot down and Flg Off C Ortmans was killed by a Ki-43 pilot as he hung in his parachute. This unsavoury practice was routinely observed by JAAF pilots throughout the war.

The 50th claimed two kills on the 2nd and six on the 4th, with a Hurricane on the latter date being credited to Sgt Anabuki. The following day, both sentais saw action as they strafed enemy airfields in an attempt to keep Allied fighters away from JAAF bombers – a handful of claims were made.

On 9 April the 64th Sentai attacked Chittagong yet again. As the 16-strong formation approached the airfield, Capt Kuroe spotted nine Hurricanes from No 67 Sqn climbing through 6500 ft in an attempt to intercept the raiders. Kuroe fired at one of them, which Sgt Miyoshi Watanabe then attacked from behind. The Hurricane raised its nose, stalled and crashed into the sea. Lt Takahashi and Sgt Watanabe then turned their attention to the aircraft flown by Sqn Ldr J Bachmann, which belched out smoke while jinking at low altitude. Kuroe finished it off with a 150-round burst, the fighter hitting a house and exploding.

The 64th claimed two victories plus two probables without any loss. 'Today's combat was almost perfect', Kuroe later confided to his diary. Sgt Watanabe was credited with a share in both Hurricanes, taking his overall tally to seven victories. Capt Kuroe's wingman, and fellow ace, Sgt Maj Yasuda also recalled the operation on 9 April;

'It went just like the combat training we practised every day. The results we achieved were very satisfying for a fighter pilot. We were inspired when we saw Capt Kuroe leave the command post smiling and with a spring in his step, even though he was very tired from the continuous air battles. He was an excellent combat leader.'

The statistics for the sustained period of aerial action over the Arakan that lasted from 14 March through to 11 April saw RAF fighter pilots claim 23 confirmed and 20 probable victories, as well as 45 enemy aircraft damaged. The JAAF, however, lost five Ki-48s, three Ki-21s and a Ki-36 to enemy action, but not a single Ki-43 according to official records. Some 23 'Oscars' were damaged to varying degrees in combat with RAF fighters, although none were lost. RAF losses amounted to 21 aircraft fighting with the Ki-43 – 17 Hurricanes, one Mohawk, one Beaufighter and two Blenheims. JAAF fighter pilots had flown 280 sorties between these dates, and claimed an astonishing 416 aircraft destroyed – more than the RAF's total strength in the whole of the Bengal area!

On 20 and 21 April the JAAF turned its attention to Allied targets in the Imphal, which were attacked by bombers escorted by both fighter sentais. Eight aircraft were claimed shot down by the Ki-43 units. Airfields in China were then attacked on the 26th and 28th, and two P-40Ks shot down by the 50th's Maj Ishikawa and Sgt Anabuki. Two 'Oscars' fell to the Warhawks whilst covering the bombers' withdrawal, however.

On 1 May, eight B-24s of the 492nd BS raided the port area of Rangoon. They were intercepted by four Ki-43s led by Capt Hideo Miyabe, CO of the 2nd Chutai of the 64th Sentai. The bombers, flying at just 10,000 ft, had attacked their target by the time the fighters reached them. Sgt Miyoshi Watanabe made the first pass, hitting 1Lt Robert Kavanagh's B-24 in two of its engines. Watanabe's Ki-43 was in turn struck by defensive fire on his second pass. Discovering that he was out of ammunition, and with his Ki-43 vibrating badly, Watanabe decided to ram the bomber – his propeller severed the B-24's tail turret. Despite the damage sustained by his 'Oscar', Watanabe managed to crash-land.

The B-24, meanwhile, dropped out of formation and was quickly set upon by Lt Yukimoto and WO Takahama, who shot it down into a rice paddy. The surviving crewmembers from the first B-24 to be brought down over Rangoon in daylight by the Ki-43 were captured.

Several days later, Miyabe was called to 5th Air Division headquarters, where he learned that the divisional commander had decided to decorate Watanabe for his ramming attack. Miyabe, however, felt that this would encourage further attacks and discourage teamwork. Col Miyoshi raged at Miyabe, shouting, 'We don't need advice from a chutai leader. Individual action is fine. Be reckless, make ramming attacks, do everything!' Watanabe was praised for his feat, but Miyabe's anxiety was justified, as future events would show.

While the 64th was kept busy defending Toungoo and Rangoon from increasingly frequent daylight bombing raids by USAAF squadrons, the 50th supported Japanese Army units on the Akyab front. On 4 May the sentai sent two formations over Allied lines, and they were engaged by No 135 Sqn in the morning and No 79 Sqn in the afternoon. During the latter mission, Sgt Anabuki claimed a Hurricane over the airfield at Cox's Bazaar – one of seven victories credited to the 50th that day.

On the 6th, the 64th Sentai's Lt Hirao Yukimoto caught a Lockheed F-4 Lightning of the USAAF's 9th Photographic Squadron (Light) flying below the clouds. Having damaged one of its engines, his cannon jammed during his next attack. In sheer frustration, Yukimoto flew his Ki-43 alongside the F-4 and brandished his pistol at the pilot in an attempt to get him to land the crippled aircraft at Toungoo. 2Lt Donald Humphrey chose to put the F-4 down in a rice paddy instead, and he was quickly captured.

A Ki-43-II of the 64th Sentai breaks away from a JAAF bomber over Burma during an escort mission in the spring of 1943 (*64th Sentai Association*)

Yukimoto's 'mid-air capture of an enemy aircraft' was celebrated in the Japanese press. However, by the time his family were able to stage a celebration in his hometown, Yukimoto had been killed in action. His Ki-43 had been damaged by defensive fire from a B-24 on 11 May, and when he attempted an emergency landing, the fighter, trailing fuel, burst into flames.

On 7 April it was the 64th Sentai's turn to again suffer at the hands of the B-24s. The Ki-43 pilots failed to destroy any of the marauding bombers, and one fighter was damaged badly enough to necessitate a crash-landing and another Ki-43 pilot had to take to his parachute. Some pilots who had failed to catch the bombers expressed the hope that their Ki-43s would be replaced by the later Ki-44 Type 2 fighter, which was faster and had greater firepower.

15 May saw both sentais escort 30 Ki-48s that were sent to attack the USAAF base at Kunming, and although the Ki-43 pilots were credited with nine P-40s destroyed (none were lost), no fewer than four pilots were killed in return. Amongst the latter was the 64th Sentai's 3rd Chutai leader Lt Takeshi Endo. The 50th also lost a pilot over Meiktila.

Six days later, 17 64th Sentai Ki-43s led by Kuroe, together with 13 from the 50th led by Maj Nitta, raided the airfield at Cox's Bazaar. The 64th's machines flew below the overcast, while those of the 50th kept above it. Kuroe led his Ki-43s out to sea before turning inland for a low-level pass over the target. Eight-victory ace 2Lt Naoyuki Ito recalled;

'It was the perfect surprise attack. We encountered no anti-aircraft fire, but we could find no worthwhile targets. We were circling at 3250 ft when I saw Capt Kuroe's formation climb.'

Kuroe had spotted two Hurricanes, but when he penetrated the overcast in pursuit of one of them, he encountered two more. One dived to escape and he chased it. They went down to low level and the Hurricane jinked over the treetops, but there was no escape and Kuroe shot it down – two more Hurricanes were claimed by other 64th Sentai pilots. No 79 Sqn lost two Hurricanes. The sentai had not finished yet, however. It initially turned away, but then returned to surprise a No 11 Sqn Blenheim, which fell victim to Lt Takahashi.

On the return flight, the 64th encountered nine B-25s of the USAAF's 490th BS flying at 11,400 ft. Lt Goon's B-25 was shot down but four crewmembers were able to bale out, although three were killed during their descent. Eight-kill ace 2Lt Naoyuki Ito recalled;

'I aimed at one of the escaping crewmembers but my wing tip accidentally caught his parachute canopy. I was reprimanded by Capt Kuroe after we landed. He told me, "It was thoughtless. You might have become caught up in the canopy".'

On 29 May, just before the start of the monsoon season, nine Ki-43s from the 64th and 15 from the 50th Sentais were escorting 12 Ki-48s when they engaged 21 Hurricanes of Nos 67 and 136 Sqns over the target. Ramming hero Sgt Watanabe went after a diving Hurricane but chased it too far alone and did not return. Miyabe's earlier concern that he might take such reckless action in future had now been justified. On the plus side, Sgt Anabuki claimed yet another Hurricane destroyed.

All told, the 64th Sentai had lost 19 Ki-43s and 15 pilots in combat between 9 September 1942 and 29 May 1943, with the 50th losing 16 fighters and 11 pilots. Allied records show that Hurricane pilots claimed nine Ki-43s, P-40 pilots ten, P-36 pilots five, B-24 gunners five and Blenheim gunners two. Four Ki-43s fell to flak. In return, 36 Hurricanes were shot down by Ki-43s and 25 pilots killed. The Allies also lost five P-36s, five B-24s, five Blenheims, three P-40s, two B-25s, one Beaufighter, one Hudson, one Wellington and one F-4 to Ki-43s.

With the monsoon season petering out by early September, aerial combat resumed once again on the Burma front. The Japanese still had their sights on India, whilst Allied forces were adamant that they would retain a toehold in northern Burma. Supporting their efforts against the JAAF were new fighters in the form of the P-38G, P-51A and Spitfire V.

Having spent the monsoon months in the East Indies (as had the 50th Sentai), the 64th Sentai claimed its first kill over Burma since late May on 10 September, when old hand Sgt Maj Shigeru Takuwa surprised an F-4 over Rangoon. Three days later, Capt Kuroe bagged another reconnaissance machine when he destroyed a newer F-5A Lightning. Although the latter machine was considerably faster than his Ki-43, Kuroe doggedly maintained his pursuit. After 30 minutes, he was right behind the twin-boom machine, and he eventually shot it down. The Japanese fighter pilots were well aware that if they failed to destroy these reconnaissance aircraft, the B-24s would follow the very next day.

On 2 October, 18 50th Sentai Ki-43s returned to Mingaladon from Malaya and prepared for action. The unit intercepted 22 B-24s on the 4th, but none were brought down. 1st Chutai leader Capt Yoshihiro Takanarita was killed by the bombers' defensive fire, however, this pilot having shot down two 380th BG B-24s at Babo on 10 July 1943 while on detachment in New Guinea.

8 October saw the greatest feat in individual flying skill, and bravery, officially attributed to a Ki-43 pilot when leading JAAF ace Sgt Satoshi

These brand new Ki-43-IIs were issued to the 64th Sentai's 2nd Chutai during the unit's seasonal break in Palembang in August 1943. JAAF units moved to bases in the East Indies during the monsoon season because bad weather prevented air operations from being flown over Burma (*64th Sentai Association*)

Anabuki downed two P-38s and three B-24s. Eleven Ki-43s had scrambled at 1215 hrs after the 50th Sentai's 1st Chutai received the order 'Five heavies over Bassein at 16,000 ft. Fly east'. Encountering drop tank trouble that left him trailing behind the rest of the formation, Anabuki spotted 11 B-24s, escorted by two P-38s, in hazy conditions near Rangoon. Taking them on single-handedly, he proceeded to claim two P-38s and two B-24s shot down, before ramming a third Liberator after he had exhausted his ammunition. Anabuki, who had also been wounded in the action, then landed his battered fighter on a beach and was eventually rescued.

Newly promoted MSgt Maj Satoshi Anabuki strikes a fighter pilot's pose between Ki-43-IIIs of the Akeno Fighter School in late 1944. He is wearing the standard JAAF summer flight suit, over which he has donned a Type 92 parachute harness. The white label on the latter's strapping reads MSgt Maj Anabuki. Despite being dressed in a summer suit, the ace is inexplicably wearing a winter flying helmet. Anabuki was posted home in February 1944 after completing 173 missions in Burma (*Yasuho Izawa*)

This feat earned him an individual citation from 3rd Air Force CO Lt Gen Hideyoshi Kawabe, and promotion to sergeant major. Such citations were usually awarded posthumously, and Anabuki was the sole exception in the Imperial Japanese forces. But there had been no witnesses to his feat, and the author has been unable to find matching Allied loss reports. Veteran 64th Sentai ace Lt Naoyuki Ito was sceptical. 'A Ki-43 carried only 250 cannon rounds per gun, so it was impossible for anyone to have shot down two P-38s and three B-24s with such little ammunition', he told the author.

It is possible, however, that the JAAF's 3rd Air Force was badly in need of a hero, since the B-24s had been able to bomb any target in its sector virtually with impunity, and Anabuki fitted the bill. His success came at a price though, for he was now prohibited from engaging in any further operational flying. Anabuki's tally now stood at 30 kills (27 with the Ki-43).

On the night of 9 October, a real hero against the hitherto impregnable B-24 did indeed emerge. Three Ki-43s led by Capt Miyabe scrambled after being alerted that three Liberator bombers were over Akyab.

As they approached Rangoon, Sgt Maj Daisuke Nishizawa spotted a zigzagging B-24 caught in a searchlight beam. He attempted a head-on pass, opening fire just as the bomber lifted its nose to avoid colliding with the fighter. Nishizawa hit the bomber's inboard left-hand engine, and he saw flames erupt from the wing root. The 'Oscar' pilot then banked around and made another head-on pass, sending the Liberator down trailing flame until its bomb load exploded 1000 ft above the ground. The B-24 illuminated the night sky over the city, and its wreckage was later found in a rice paddy.

While the 64th attempted to blunt USAAF day and night missions against Rangoon, the 50th Sentai was given an equally important task by the 5th Air Division. Eight Ki-43s, led by 2Lt Toshio Yamashita, were detached from Mingaladon to Myitkyina, in northeastern Burma, on 12 October. The following morning, they departed on the first Operation *Tsujigiri* (Street Murder) mission performed by the JAAF. Their objective was to intercept Allied transport aircraft that were flying between Assam and China on the 'over-the-Hump' route. Evading Allied fighters, the 'Oscar' pilots claimed three transports destroyed – a C-46, a C-47 and a C-87 (the cargo variant of the B-24). However, bomb-carrying P-40Ns of the 88th FS soon located the Japanese fighters at Myitkyina and forced the 50th to withdraw its Ki-43s south to Mingaladon.

A more routine operation was conducted on 20 October after the crew of a Ki-46 reconnaissance aircraft reported that Allied ships were assembling in Chittagong harbour. The JAAF's 5th Air Division ordered an attack, which was the first such mission of the 'shooting season'. Nineteen Ki-21s of the 12th and 98th Sentais were given the job of attacking the naval vessels, and they would be escorted by 14 Ki-43s from the 64th Sentai. The 50th Sentai would fly an advanced fighter sweep.

Hurricanes attempted to intercept the twin-engined bombers as they approached Chittagong, but they were driven off by the Ki-43s. Three No 261 Sqn aircraft were downed, and for once RAF losses matched JAAF claims, with the 'Oscar' pilots stating that three Hurricanes had been destroyed. No Ki-43s were lost, although for a while ace 2Lt Naoyuki Ito of the 64th Sentai and Sgt Maj Takuwa were both missing. Ito had chased a Hurricane too far west on his own and missed his quarry. Trailed by two or three other RAF fighters, he turned to attack them and fired at one that disappeared into the valley streaming white smoke.

When both pilots failed to return to base, it was feared that they had run out of fuel. However, they eventually appeared over Mingaladon, and in spite of their shortage of fuel, both men dived at the runway before zooming up again – the victory signal. Ito and Takuwa each claimed a Hurricane destroyed.

The 50th flew another *Tsujigiri* mission on 23 October, when Ki-43 pilots sortied from Myitkyina in two groups of four and intercepted Allied transport aircraft over Sumprabum at 10,000 ft. In just an hour they claimed three 'DC-2s' destroyed and damaged a C-87. The USAAF's Air Transport Command lost three more C-47s.

Despite these successes in northern Burma, in the south, B-24s continued to be the Ki-43 pilots' most feared opponent, as the JAAF was unable to provide additional means of dealing with these heavy bombers bristling with defensive machine guns. With no replacement aircraft in the offing, Capt Kuroe and his men quickly realised that they would have to rely on their fighting spirit and courage, as well as their skill, to defeat the B-24s. 1st Chutai leader Lt Saburo Nakamura attempted to rally his men with a rousing speech. 'When I'm in the Hayabusa', he told them, 'nothing can shoot me down – not even a dozen enemy fighters. I'll punch any pilot who takes hits from enemy fighters in a dogfight. I'll also punch any pilot who *doesn't* take hits while attacking enemy bombers!'

It was one of the youngest and least experienced pilots in the 64th who lived up to this exhortation. On 24 October, Cpl Tomio Kamiguchi rammed a B-24 from the 492nd BS and was forced to take to his parachute. JAAF 5th Air Division CO Maj Gen Tanaka praised him highly, and the feat was widely reported in the Japanese press. He became a hero, being dubbed 'Corporal Saw' because he had cut up the B-24 with his propeller. Not everybody was impressed, however. 'It wasn't necessary' 2Lt Naoyuki Ito told the author, pointing out that the B-24 had already been fatally damaged by other Ki-43s before Kamiguchi rammed it. 'It would have been

A victory smile from the 64th Sentai's leading ace, Capt Yasuhiko Kuroe, who had just returned to base after downing a PR Mosquito from No 684 Sqn over Mingaladon on 2 November 1943 – the first Mosquito to be destroyed by a JAAF fighter. The wreckage of the aircraft was duly sent to Japan to enable its wooden construction to be studied. Capt Kuroe, who was credited with two Soviet fighters destroyed during the Nomonhan Incident, scored his next three kills flying pre-production Ki-44s with the Dokuhi 47th (47th Independent Flying) Chutai in Malaya and Burma. He was then transferred to the 64th Sentai as its 3rd Chutai leader in April 1942, and Kuroe had taken his tally to 27 kills by the time he returned to Japan in January 1944. Claiming three more victories whilst serving with the Army Flight Test Centre in 1945, Kuroe survived the war and later served as a fighter pilot with the Japanese Self-Defence Air Force until he was accidentally killed during a fishing accident in November 1965 (*64th Sentai Association*)

very difficult, if not impossible, for him to have rammed the B-24 if all of its guns had been in action', he said.

Ito's old friend Sgt Maj Takuwa, who was acting as a mentor to the younger pilots, tried to calm them down. 'We were worried that our young aviators would follow Kamiguchi's reckless action', Ito recalled.

The 50th Sentai attempted its third *Tsujigiri* mission on 27 October. In an effort to frustrate the Ki-43 pilots, the Allies had moved the routes flown by their transport aircraft further north. But the JAAF pilots who took off from Loiwing airfield that morning returned from their mission claiming to have shot down a 'DC-3' – Air Transport Command admitted the loss of a C-46. In the afternoon, four Ki-43s led by 3rd Chutai leader Capt Shigeharu Hashimoto spotted two formations of three B-24s. Lt Noriyuki Saito jettisoned his drop tank and followed Hashimoto, who flew into the heavy defensive fire as he attacked the bombers from head-on.

Pilots of the 50th Sentai had already shot down or damaged unarmed C-87s in this area, but now their opponents were B-24s of the 308th BG. Carrying additional ammunition instead of bombs, their crews had been ordered to fly low to fool the *Tsujigiri* pilots into thinking that they were C-87s. It was legendary Fourteenth Air Force commander Gen Claire Chennault who had ordered that the B-24s be transformed into huge fighters in order to prevent the *Tsujigiri* missions from obstructing this vital supply route to China. The Liberator gunners claimed to have shot down no fewer than 18 Ki-43s on this mission, although actual losses amounted to three fighters and two pilots. All the B-24s returned home, having once again proved their ability to outgun the Ki-43s.

Shortly after this mission, the increasingly hard-pressed fighter force in Burma was bolstered by the arrival of the 33rd Sentai. Equipped with Ki-43-IIs, the unit had been based in China since 1937. Its stay in Burma would be brief, however, as it was posted to New Guinea in early 1944.

On 2 November, Capt Kuroe took off with 2Lt Ito to intercept a No 684 Sqn PR Mosquito as the aircraft flew a reconnaissance mission over Rangoon. The pair circled at 29,000 ft, and after a while the two Japanese aircraft became separated, but Kuroe spotted the target and climbed to 30,000 ft in order to get above it. He then dived onto the tail of the Mosquito without being spotted and shot the aircraft down.

On the 11th, Lt Mamoru Furue led four 50th Sentai Ki-43s in an interception of 7th BG B-24s over

Heho airfield at 6500 ft. Although they were only able to claim to have damaged three or four of the attackers, two badly damaged 9th BS Liberators force-landed at Chittagong. Three crewmembers had been killed in the attacks and four others wounded. In the wake of this seemingly unsuccessful mission, Furue resolved to make a do or die effort to destroy the marauding 'heavies'. He got his chance three days later.

Seven Ki-43s from the 50th were scrambled as a formation of heavy bombers was sighted west of Shwebo. The first flight of four Ki-43s was led by Lt Takashi Tomomune, while the second, of three fighters, was headed up by Lt Furue. They climbed to 22,750 ft and spotted 12 B-24Js of the 493rd BS/7th BG cruising over the green mountains below them. They seemed intent on attacking Heho airfield. Future 19-kill ace Sgt Maj Yojiro Ohbusa of Furue's flight waggled his wings and pointed out the bomber formation to his leader.

Lt Takashi Tomomune (in his summer flying suit) of the 50th Sentai led a flight of four Ki-43s against 12 B-24Js of the 493rd BS/ 7th BG on 14 November 1943. Two Ki-43s and one pilot were lost to intense defensive fire, but the 493rd BS suffered a severe mauling nonetheless (*Yasuho Izawa*)

The B-24s were flying in two separate groups of five and seven. The larger one maintained course for Heho, while the other five turned west. When Furue and his Ki-43s approached, the seven B-24s jettisoned their bombs and headed for Pakokku.

Furue led his men in a head-on attack from 1300 yards, diving at them from a height of 800 ft above the bombers. Sgt Maj Ohbusa aimed at the right-hand tail-end B-24 and watched as his fire hit its right inner engine. He broke away as a stream of red tracers spewed from its belly turret.

The second flight formed up in line astern for the next attack on Ohbusa's B-24, which was trailing white smoke. Sgt Sato was now leading the fighters, with Ohbusa 200 m astern and Furue a further 100 m behind him. When Ohbusa rushed into the attack, he saw a white parachute floating behind the B-24 being attacked by Sato. He aimed at the outer right engine of the bomber trailing white smoke and felt defensive fire hitting his fighter. Smoke and flames filled his cockpit when he broke away, forcing him to bale out with severe burns.

The Japanese fighter pilots had managed to shoot down three B-24s, but lost three of their number in return. Ten bomber crewmembers were taken prisoner, and the outcome of the battle convinced the USAAF that unescorted B-24 operations were now too costly to continue with.

Despite these losses, the Allies planned a strategic bombing offensive against Rangoon. This commenced on 25 November, when 30 B-24s of the 7th and 308th BGs, escorted by six newly arrived P-51As of the 311th Fighter-Bomber Group (FBG), rendezvoused over Ramu. Heavy cloud prevented the bombers from meeting up with their escorts, however.

At that time the air defence of Rangoon consisted of just ten Ki-43s from the 64th Sentai's 3rd Chutai. Four of them, led by ace Lt Yohei Hinoki, scrambled when the air raid warning came in on the 25th. Instead of encountering now familiar B-24s, the pilots intercepted a

50th Sentai ace Sgt Maj Yojiro Ohbusa was also involved in the 14 November B-24 intercept, which saw two 493rd BS bombers shot down. However, Ohbusa's aircraft was hit so severely by defensive fire that he too had to take to his parachute. He claimed 19 kills and survived the war (*Yasuho Izawa*)

formation of unidentified inline-engined fighters flying at 13,000 ft. These were the first Allied fighters seen over the Japanese-held city for almost two years.

Future 27-kill ace Lt Goichi Sumino, who had been aloft instructing novice fighter pilots, spotted the aircraft and climbed towards the formation alone. A P-51 quickly got in behind the 'Oscar' and shot it up. Hinoki rushed to rescue his friend, firing a burst at the formation leader, Lt James England. His wingman, 2Lt Lockett, dived to escape Hinoki's wingmen, Sgt Maj Toba and WO Tadashi Kinoshita. An old hand, Kinoshita chased Lockett for 125 miles before the Mustang slowed sufficiently for him to attack it over Bassein from behind and below. The fighter crashed onto a sandbar at the junction of two rivers.

That same afternoon, eight P-51As returned to the city. They reported encountering ten Ki-43s and six Ki-45 twin-engined fighters, and the lead Mustang was so badly hit by Hinoki that its pilot had to bale out and he was made a PoW. All told, the 311th FBG lost two P-51As and two pilots in its first duel with the older, but battle-hardened, Ki-43 pilots.

On his return, Hinoki reported to Kuroe, 'The new fighters are escorting the B-25s. They're much faster than our Hayabusas. When we attack them from above they just fly away right out of range. We're no problem at all for them'. At their home base, the returning P-51 pilots spoke about their meeting with skilful, but not too aggressive, 'Black Dragon' fighters over Rangoon.

Several hours later, 13 RAF Wellingtons from No 215 Sqn attacked Mahlwagon. In a rare night interception, Ki-43s of the 64th Sentai's 3rd Chutai claimed two of them shot down. One belly-landed at its home base and another crashed on approach.

On the 27th, 56 B-24s took off for the second strike on Rangoon, escorted by five P-51As and four P-38Js of the 459th FS. A further attack was mounted by nine B-25s of the 341st BG, escorted by ten P-51As. Only eight Ki-43s and one Ki-44 from the 64th Sentai's 3rd Chutai, together with Ki-45s of the 21st Sentai's 1st Chutai, were available to face this armada of 84 Allied bombers and fighters. Kuroe ordered his men to attack the escorting fighters first.

As they climbed to intercept, JAAF ground control directed them towards the raiders, and they encountered a large formation at 16,000 ft. The first flight of four Ki-43s went into line-astern formation and attacked the P-38s flying over the bombers. Hinoki's fire set one of the twin-boom fighters ablaze, while another tried to jink to the left. Kuroe fired at a second Lightning, which belched white smoke. After a burst from his wingman, he noticed Capt Armin Ortmeyer and 2Lt Jay Harlan escaping from their burning P-38s.

Capt Kuroe then went after a flight of four P-51As flying above the B-24s, but he was forced to break away when they all turned into him. Once the Mustangs had resumed their escort duty, Kuroe made a bold dash at them at full throttle. The P-51s were flying at cruising speed, with their drop tanks still attached, and the JAAF ace opened fire on the fourth aircraft in the formation from a range of 150 yards. Bursting into flames, it crashed 25 miles west of Rangoon.

Lt Hinoki, meanwhile, chased a formation of B-24s for more than 250 km. He was accompanied by Cpl Teizo Yamamoto, who eventually

Tenacious ace Lt Yohei Hinoki returned to Burma from a chutai leader's course in April 1943. He became 3rd Chutai leader the following month after Lt Takeshi Endo was killed in action. Like many JAAF officers, Hinoki would often carry his sword with him in his aircraft for good luck. Hinoki's flight helmet was a gift from his flying instructor, Nomonhan Incident nine-kill ace Maj Iori Sakai (*Yohei Hinoki*)

rushed into the bombers' defensive fire and crashed in flames. Hinoki jumped one of four escorting P-51s and shot it down. He then made a head-on pass at the tail-end B-24 of the 308th BG, before returning to attack the bomber from the rear.

Having knocked out one of its engines, Hinoki was then set upon by future ace 2Lt Bob Mulhollem of the 530th FBS. The Ki-43 was badly shot up and the ace was struck by a single 0.50-in round that all but severed his right leg. Somehow escaping his opponent, who had already claimed two 'Oscars' destroyed in this mission, Hinoki limped back to base. His leg was amputated shortly afterwards, and he then spent many months in hospital regaining sufficient strength in order to survive being shipped back to Japan. Hinoki eventually returned to flying duties with an artificial leg, at first instructing at the Akeno Fighter School and then successfully piloting Ki-84s and Ki-100s in the defence of Japan.

Whilst Hinoki was dogfighting with Mulhollem, Kuroe was also engaging P-51s. He had spotted eight Mustangs escorting nine B-25s some way off, and decided to attack them. Kuroe fired at the tail-end P-51A and it burst into flames and crashed west of Rangoon. Moments later he was chasing another Mustang that had suddenly dived out of formation. Despite the P-51A's superior speed, Kuroe began a determined low-level pursuit. The P-51 was zig-zagging while Kuroe was gradually closing in. Finally, a well-aimed three-second burst had the Mustang streaming white smoke and crash-landing in the swamp below.

The 311th FBG had lost four P-51As and their pilots, while the 459th FS reported losing two P-38s and their pilots. In addition, three B-24s failed to return and five others were damaged. The 64th Sentai lost a Ki-44 to a P-51A and a Ki-43 to defensive fire from a B-24.

In late November the Ki-43-II-equipped 204th Hiko Sentai was transferred to Mingaladon from Kashiwa, in China, and it would subsequently fight on the Burma front until posted to the Philippines in October 1944. Its arrival coincided with the massing of JAAF fighter units at airfields in the Rangoon area in preparation for a large-scale raid on Calcutta – the key Allied base for the Burma campaign, as well as a supply hub in support of the war in China.

Allied reconnaissance flights detected this build up, and B-24s attacked various bases in Rangoon on 1 December. More than 50 fighters – Ki-45s of the 21st Sentai, together with Ki-43s from the 64th and 204th Sentais – took off to intercept. Among them was future 12-kill ace Cpl Toshimi Ikezawa of the 64th Sentai, who recalled;

'It was my first taste of action. Lt Sanae Ishii was killed in this battle. He climbed from a lower altitude to attack the B-24s head-on, but his Ki-43 nearly stalled when he turned to break away. The Liberators concentrated their fire on him – it couldn't have been any worse. That day the sky was literally full of bombers. We would face another formation as soon as we had completed a head-on pass on the previous one, forcing us to turn rapidly for the next attack.

'We were taught to attack head-on from above, diving to gain speed and closing the distance as quickly as we could. But it was terrifying! I used to start firing from 540 yards, then break at between 220 to 325 yards, but I felt that I was probably too far away to be effective.'

Fellow ace 2Lt Naoyuki Ito was also involved in this action;

NCO pilots of the 64th Sentai/3rd Chutai pose for the camera in front of the Ki-43 of chutai leader Capt Yohei Hinoki at Mingaladon airfield. These newly-joined pilots, fresh from a training school in Japan, got their first taste of combat over Rangoon on 1 December 1943 when airfields in and around the Burmese capital were bombed by B-24s (*Yoji Watanabe*)

'I found that the climbing head-on attack was best. It reduced speed so I could aim at the bomber at will. On 1 December I made my first pass on a B-24 just as an anti-aircraft battery opened fire. I could see some hits, but the B-24 seemed to be flying all right. The formation made a wide left turn after they had completed their attack. We made a tight turn and went far ahead of them. I then came in and attacked the right-hand tail-end B-24.

'My field of vision was filled with tracers coming at me like countless red balls as my own rounds mixed with defensive fire from the bombers. I felt my tail shudder when I pushed the control column forward to break away. I saw that my wings were riddled with holes and leaking fuel. I turned off my engine to prevent a fire and glided down to land at one of Rangoon's satellite airfields. The top of my vertical stabiliser had gone, and there were bullet holes all over my Ki-43.'

Capt Kuroe watched Lt Kurosawa's element make a head-on pass on the leading B-24 of the second formation. It was engulfed in flames, and the rest of the formation scattered. Kuroe then flew ahead of another Liberator, before turning to make a head-on pass. He was able to gain hits, but felt his own aircraft start to vibrate – an undercarriage leg had extended after becoming unlocked. He then spotted a large hole in his elevator and noticed that he had lost the aileron from his left wing.

WO Kinoshita and WO Yamashita duly attacked Kuroe's B-24 but ran out of ammunition. The bomber was still flying, albeit so slowly that even Kuroe's crippled Ki-43 could catch it, and he watched it crash.

The JAAF had lost two 64th Sentai machines to defensive fire from the B-24s, with several others damaged. The JAAF claimed to have shot down ten B-24s (two by the 204th Sentai), two P-51s and a P-38. The USAAF acknowledged the loss of five B-24s from the 7th BG and one from the 308th BG, whilst the 311th FBG had a P-51A shot down.

The 7th and 308th BGs, as well as the RAF's No 215 Sqn, flew 222 sorties against Rangoon and other targets during the strategic bombing offensive, which ran from 25 November to 1 December 1943. Their losses were 12 B-24s, eight P-51As, two P-38Js and three Wellingtons. JAAF losses were four Ki-43s, one Ki-44 and one Ki-45. Many more fighters were damaged and put out of action for a time, however.

The Japanese struck back with a raid on Calcutta on 5 December, the JAAF despatching 18 Ki-21s escorted by 74 Ki-43s from the 33rd, 50th and 64th Sentais. IJN G4M 'Betty' bombers and A6M Zero-sens also participated in this mission, which was deemed to be a success as various targets were hit for the loss of just one Ki-21. The RAF had six Hurricanes shot down and four pilots killed by the escorting fighters, which were joined by the 204th during the return leg of the mission.

On 10 December, Capt Kuroe caught a No 684 Sqn Mosquito during a reconnaissance mission over Rangoon. After a pursuit lasting 40 minutes, Kuroe was able to damage one of the Mosquito's engines, but then his cannon jammed. Flying alongside the crippled aircraft, he saw a white cloth being waved from its cockpit. Kuroe tried to force the crew to land at a JAAF airfield at Rangoon but the Mosquito crashed, killing both the pilot and navigator. It was Kuroe's final success in Burma.

That same day the 50th Sentai claimed five *Tsujigiri* victories, whilst the 33rd escorted bombers to Fort Hertz and were credited with four kills for the loss of three Ki-43s. On the 13th, this sentai, along with the 50th and 204th, claimed 18 victories when they covered bombers sent to attack Tinsukia. The 204th lost two Ki-43s, but were also credited with half of the kills. Escort missions on the 18th and 19th saw 15 more victories credited to the 33rd, 50th and 64th as the JAAF turned its attention to targets in southern China.

1943 ended for the Ki-43 units with a series of missions to China and northern Burma, as Japanese bombers attempted to keep Allied advances on the ground in check. Nine fighters were lost during missions flown on 22, 26 and 31 December, although the 33rd, 64th and 204th Sentais claimed 34 kills between them! The 'Oscar' units had done well throughout the year, but the advent of P-51s, P-38s and, in late December, Spitfire Vs, now found the sentais very much up against it as the conflict entered its third year. And unlike their Allied counterparts, the JAAF pilots had no new fighters waiting in the wings to help restore the aerial balance of power in their favour.

When the RAF's Burma-based fighter squadrons started converting to Spitfire Vs and VIIIs, their pilots rejoiced in the types' extra performance in comparison with the Hurricane II. By contrast, JAAF pilots were disappointed in the new late-production Ki-43-II, which was some 15 mph slower than the previous version because of the additional wind resistance caused by the new drop tank installations.

Cpl Toshimi Ikezawa, who claimed 12 kills with the 64th Sentai in Burma, recalled an early encounter that he had with Spitfires;

'When a "Spit" attacked from below, we would dive to attack it. When the enemy noticed that, he'd lower his nose, then zoom right up in no time, far above us. The Spitfires were so much better than our Ki-43s.'

Cpl Toshimi Ikezawa of the 64th Sentai's 1st Chutai was a young and aggressive fighter pilot just like Sgt Miyoshi Watanabe. Tending to rush into individual combats, most of Ikezawa's 12 aerial claims can be corroborated by Allied loss reports (*Toshimi Ikezawa*)

The new Spitfires were intended to secure air superiority for the Second Arakan Campaign, which involved the 5th and 7th Indian Divisions, together with the West African Division, advancing along the Arakan coast towards Akyab. The vital city of Maungdaw fell on 9 January.

In response to this offensive, the 64th Sentai moved to Meiktila airfield on the 14th, from where its pilots patrolled the Irrawaddy River but found no Allied aircraft. The unit planned a more aggressive mission for the following day, with each chutai flying an hour-long sweep over the frontline from Akyab to Maungdow. The first was undertaken by eight Ki-43s of the 3rd Chutai, led by Lt Sumino. They were soon detected by RAF radar south of the Kalapanzin Valley, and 25 Spitfires of Nos 136 and 607 Sqns were scrambled. Ground control vectored them into a favourable attacking position as the Ki-43s were southwest of Teknaf. Eight-kill ace 2Lt Naoyuki Ito remembered what happened next;

'When we were circling, searching for the enemy, my radio became noisy. I heard English voices, and at the same time sighted some 20 Spitfires in the sun. I waggled my wings to alert the others.'

When a Spitfire opened fire from long range, Ito broke away to the left to avoid it. The next moment another Spitfire fired at him from the right. He avoided it too and zoomed upwards. Ito chased the Spitfire and fired a burst at it, then did a quick roll. He narrowly avoided colliding with the RAF fighter, which crashed into the River Kalapanzin.

Both squadrons claimed five victories, three probables and three damaged. Flg Off Fuge of No 136 Sqn was killed and Flg Off Garvan of the same unit belly-landed in a rice paddy and was rescued. The 3rd Chutai claimed to have shot down four Spitfires for the loss of a solitary Ki-43.

The second sweep of the day was flown by eight Ki-43s of the 1st Chutai, and they encountered Spitfires of No 607 Sqn over Buthidaung at 19,500 ft. Five Ki-43s were providing top cover at the time for three other fighters that were strafing ground targets. The latter machines were shot down, killing the highly-experienced Sgt Maj Shigeru Takuwa and newcomer Cpl Mikio Kondo. Lt Hokyo baled out, but he was killed either by a Spitfire while in his parachute or by the failure of his canopy to deploy in time. Toshimi Ikezawa recalled;

'I think Sgt Maj Takuwa was killed while attempting to cover Cpl Kondo. He was a veteran of 100 battles, and he would never have been killed if he hadn't been trying to save someone else. He used to look after all of us younger pilots. His death was a bitter experience for me.'

The Spitfires of No 136 Sqn spotted the third sweep by eight Ki-43s of the 2nd Chutai, led by Capt Miyabe. Again, an 'Oscar' was lost, although the survivors claimed four enemy aircraft destroyed (only a solitary Hurricane of No 6 Sqn Indian Air Force was actually downed that day).

The 64th Sentai had had five pilots killed during the course of a single day, which was the biggest defeat it had suffered to date. For its part, the RAF had defeated each chutai and claimed to have accounted for 16 aircraft, with five reported as probables and 18 damaged. These scores made front-page news in Calcutta.

Overclaiming remained rife in Burma during this period, with the 50th Sentai being credited with seven kills on the 18 January and the 204th 20 P-51s and Spitfires over Akyab two days later! The 77th Sentai also claimed five C-47s during a series of *Tsujigiri* missions along the 'Hump' route from Maymyo, prior to heading to New Guinea (along with the 33rd Sentai) at month-end. Just three Ki-43 sentais now remained in Burma.

On 4 February, some 70 Ki-43s of the 50th, 64th and 204th Sentais concentrated over Maungdaw to provide air support for the Japanese Army's 55th Division as it advanced in preparation for a counter-attack at Taung Bazar. While the Spitfires of No 136 Sqn were doing their best to avoid the overwhelming force of Ki-43s, 2Lt Naoyuki Ito of the 64th Sentai spotted a Hurricane far below him heading north. After a long dive, he fired a burst at it, but Ito found it hard to aim with any accuracy due to his excessive closing speed. He broke away so as to avoid colliding with his target, leaving the No 6 Sqn fighter to be shot down by the 204th Sentai's leading ace, Lt Hiroshi Gomi. The latter had shot a Spitfire off the tail of his chutai leader earlier in the mission.

The 64th and 204th Sentais claimed 15 victories that day, but the Hurricane was the only confirmed Allied loss.

Having been trained alongside fellow ace Shogo Takeuchi in 1937-39, Koki Kawamoto served as a fighter instructor in China and Japan before being posted to the 50th Sentai as a hikotai leader in October 1943. Seeing action for the first time on the Calcutta raid of 5 December 1943, Kawamoto also claimed victories during *Tsujigiri* missions undertaken by the 50th Sentai in early 1944. Promoted to major in December of that year, he became the 50th Sentai's final CO following the death of Maj Tatsujiro Fujii in March 1945. Kawamoto survived the war with eight victories to his credit (*Yasuho Izawa*)

The next day, three sentais returned to fight the RAF, which lost a No 136 Sqn Spitfire and two Hurricanes from No 11 Sqn. Over two days of fighting the Ki-43 pilots had accounted for one Spitfire and three Hurricanes without loss to themselves.

The 64th tangled with Hurricanes again on 8 February, and leading ace Lt Goichi Sumino was in the process of shooting one down when he had a cannon round explode in the breech of one of his guns, forcing him to crash-land. His success on this mission was his 25th claim on the Burma front.

The 50th Sentai was temporarily assigned to fly fighter sweeps over the railway line between Indaw and Kawlin on 13-14 February so as to prevent it from being bombed and strafed by B-25s and P-51As of the newly arrived 1st Air Commando Group (ACG). Although the Ki-43 pilots were unable to find enemy aircraft on the 13th, they encountered 13 Mustangs the next day. The unit's pilots claimed to have downed eight US aircraft, but just two P-51As were in fact lost – among those credited with kills were ranking sentai aces WOs Isamu Sasaki and Yojiro Ohbusa.

64th Sentai aces enjoyed success on 18 February, when Cpl Toshimi Ikezawa claimed his first victory when he shared in the destruction of a No 20 Sqn Hurricane IID with Lt Naoyuki Ito. 'I was Ito's wingman', Ikezawa recalled, 'and turned and dived towards a Hurricane flying below us. When he fired a burst at it, it streamed fuel. The next moment, I rushed in to fire at the Hurricane and set it afire'. The 64th claimed two Hurricanes that day.

It was the 204th Sentai's turn to 'mix it' with the RAF on 21 February, when its pilots claimed to have shot down eight Spitfires over Kaladan (No 136 Sqn actually lost two aircraft). The 204th then encountered two Hurricanes of No 6 Sqn IAF and shot one of them down.

Despite these victories, growing Allied air power in-theatre ensured success in the second Akyab (Arakan) campaign, which in turn represented the Japanese Army's first defeat in Burma. On 23 February, the 55th Division was forced to retreat, despite encircling the 5th and 7th Indian divisions, both of which had to be resupplied from the air. In February, JAAF fighters shot down four Spitfires, ten Hurricanes, two P-51As and a C-47. That same month the JAAF lost eight Ki-43s (and six pilots). 'Oscar' pilots scored more aerial victories than their Allied opponents, but they were unable to prevent the air supply operation.

Aces Lt Hiroshi Takiguchi and WO Bunichi Yamaguchi ended the month on a successful note for the 204th Sentai when they were scrambled during the night of 29 February/1 March to intercept eight Liberator IIIs of No 159 Sqn over Rangoon. In the darkness, each pilot fired two bursts at a bomber that had been trapped by searchlights over Mingaladon airfield, and it duly crashed. 'I don't know how many B-24s there were', Yamaguchi later recalled. 'Fortunately, the first one was caught by our searchlights'.

The Hayabusa pilots then spotted a second Liberator III struggling to escape the glare of the searchlights, and it too crashed when hit by bursts from both fighters. Takiguchi and Yamaguchi attacked two more bombers when they too were framed in the searchlight beam, but these escaped. No 159 Sqn lost two Liberator IIIs, and a third one from No 355 Sqn was damaged.

64th Sentai/1st Chutai leader Capt Saburo Nakamura shot down a Beaufighter X of No 211 Sqn on 6 March 1944, followed by a Spitfire VIII from No 81 Sqn exactly one week later (*64th Sentai Association*)

Six Beaufighters of No 211 Sqn raided the airfields around Rangoon on 6 March, this attack being witnessed by Cpl Toshimi Ikezawa of the 64th Sentai;

'Our main force was at Hlegu airfield. Most of our Ki-43s were in blast shelters beneath the mango trees. Only four or five fighters were lined up in front of the pilots' hut. Maj Yoshio Hirose and Capt Saburo Nakamura were scrambled, and the latter shot a Beaufighter down into a bomber pen, with flames streaming from one engine.'

Ace Nakamura's scoring rival in the 64th Sentai, Lt Goichi Sumino, also enjoyed success two days later when he shot down a P-51A of the 1st ACG over Shwebo. Aces Capt Hideo Miyabe and 2Lt Norio Shindo were amongst the kills on 12 March when they shared in the destruction of two small liaison aircraft spotted at low level over Arakan Yomas. The downing of these machines resulted in 30 Spitfires being scrambled to intercept them, and Shindo claimed three fighters shot down too.

The following day, the RAF's 'Broadway' airstrip was raided by 40 bomb-toting Ki-43s of the 64th and 204th Sentais, which dropped their 50 kg weapons and strafed gliders. Four Spitfires of No 81 Sqn were scrambled, and two of them were attacked by Ki-43s just as they got airborne. 1st Chutai leader Capt Nakamura shot one down into the jungle, but the other aircraft, skilfully flown by Australian pilot Flg Off Larry Cronin, avoided every attack. The No 81 Sqn pilot eventually downed a Ki-43 from the 204th Sentai, this kill making him an ace.

On 15 March, the Japanese 15th Army launched Operation *U-Go*, with Imphal as its objective. The following day, 34 Ki-43s of the 50th, 64th and 204th Sentais attacked Allied airfields around the city. Spitfires of No 136 Sqn were scrambled to intercept them, and they shot down the 204th Sentai's Lt Toshio Ohtsubo. Lt Naoyuki Ito (promoted on 1 March) of the 64th Sentai sighted three Spitfires at 26,000 ft but, as he recalled later, 'they did not come our way. We circled two or three times over Imphal and then turned for home. Ten minutes later I saw my wingman, Sgt Maj Toba, waggle his wings. When I glanced behind, I was shocked to see Spitfires about to jump me from out of the sun'.

Ito was wounded, but he was able to return to Meiktila. From here, WO Norio Shindo duly flew him to a hospital in Rangoon, squeezing Ito into the space behind the pilot's seat of his Ki-43. Ito lost the sight of his right eye, and on recovery returned to Japan to become an instructor.

On 27 March USAAF P-51s succeeded in shooting down nine Ki-49s from the newly arrived 62nd Sentai when the unit attacked Ledo airfield. Escorting Ki-43s did their best to protect the heavy bombers, claiming 15 Mustangs destroyed.

The air battles in March 1944 would prove crucial to the outcome of the war in Burma, for Allied air forces were now able to report with confidence that they had secured air superiority over Burma. At month

2Lt Norio Shindo of the 64th Sentai's 2nd Chutai was another JAAF ace who spent several years as an instructor prior to reaching the frontline. Seeing combat for the first time over Burma in May 1943, Shindo's best day came on 12 March 1944 when he was credited with the destruction of four aircraft in one sortie. His tally stood at 13 kills by war's end (*64th Sentai Association*)

Lt Goichi Sumino, who competed with Capt Saburo Nakamura in the scoring stakes, shot down a P-51A of the 1st ACG over Shwebo on 8 March. He would become one of the 64th Sentai's top scorers, having claimed 27 victories by the time of his death on 6 June 1944 (*64th Sentai Association*)

end, the USAAF estimated that it had destroyed 177 JAAF aircraft in the air and on the ground. The actual figures were 14 Ki-43s, two Ki-46s, one Ki-48 and nine Ki-49s shot down and 30 aircraft destroyed on the ground. Allied sources state that a total of 15 aircraft – four P-51s, three P-38s, three Spitfires, two B-24s, one P-40, one Hurricane and one Beaufighter were shot down by Ki-43s.

Things got no better for the 'Oscar' units in April, for on the 2nd the 50th Sentai lost 15 fighters on the ground during an attack on

Amonkan by USAAF aircraft. Four more losses followed on 17 April, when 50 Ki-43s from all three sentais were engaged by ten P-51s and 20 Spitfires whilst escorting Ki-21s to Imphal. Losses such as these quickly affected the morale of 'Oscar' pilots in Burma, who now felt that the aircraft lacked the speed, armament and radio equipment necessary to allow them to wrest back air supremacy in-theatre.

More escort missions were flown towards the end of the month. On 25 April, 54 Ki-43s from the 50th, 64th, 204th Sentais, together with nine Ki-48s of the 8th Sentai, raided Silchar airfield. Cpl Itsuo Niwa of the 64th Sentai's 3rd Chutai saw Lt Goichi Sumino waggle his wings before they reached the target. Straining his eyes, he saw seven transport aircraft crossing the Ki-43s' flightpath. Sumino and wingman Niwa jettisoned their drop tanks and went after the C-47s. Sumino opened fire on one of the transports and broke away as Niwa hit the aircraft's right engine. It gushed black smoke and flame and crashed into a hill.

Although the transports' Spitfire escorts did their best to fend off the Ki-43s, Lt Hiroshi Takiguchi of the 204th Sentai also managed to claim

Newly-arrived 204th Sentai pilots are seen at Mingaladon in late 1943. Future aces WO Bun-ichi Yamaguchi (far left) and Lt Hiroshi Takiguchi attacked B-24s over Rangoon on the night of 29 February/1 March 1944 and shot two of them down (*Yasuho Izawa*)

Pilots of the 64th Sentai/1st Chutai pose for an official portrait at Meiktila West on 17 April 1944. They are, front row (from left to right), Lt Sato and Capt Nakamura, and second row (from left to right), WO Tadashi Kinoshita (who got a P-51A on 25 November 1943), Tsutsui, Shinohara, Cpl Mamoru Oshima, Sgt Yamamoto, Kawakami and Fujikawa. Oshima failed to return from a mission to Imphal later that day (*64th Sentai Association*)

64th Sentai pilots are briefed en masse at Mingaladon during the summer of 1944. They are (from left to right) Sentai CO Major Toyoki Eto (rear), WO Tadashi Kinoshita, WO Norio Shindo, Lt Hitoshi Ezaki, Sgt Maj Masahiro Fujikawa, unknown, Cpl Masahiro Ikeda, Lt Hiroshi Matsui, Sgt Kiyoshi Kadokura, Sgt Ryuzo Yamamoto, Sgt Shotoro Konishi, Capt Hideo Miyabe and Sgt Eiichi Hirano (64th Sentai Association)

50th Sentai ace Sgt Tomesaku Igarashi earned himself a reputation for being a 'P-38 killer' after claiming two of the twin-boom fighters destroyed on 6 June 1944. He was killed in combat with a Spitfire over Imphal 11 days later (Yasuho Izawa)

two destroyed – the USAAF's Troop Carrier Command reported the loss of five aircraft in the Imphal area that day, while No 81 Sqn claimed to have shot down a Ki-43. The aircraft of Lt Takashi Sato of the 64th Sentai was so badly damaged that he radioed he was going to dive to his death. He was posted missing over the Arakan mountains.

During May it was clear that the Imphal offensive had failed, although the Ki-43 units continued to be heavily involved supporting troops on the ground. Indeed, significant aerial victories were only claimed on the 19th (seven by the 64th) 25th and 29th, when all three units were credited with seven and six victories between them. Amongst the pilots to score kills was ace Capt Goichi Sumino of the 64th, who single-handedly fought five P-38s over the Arakan Yomas on 15 May and claimed one shot down, before suffering a flesh wound to his left arm.

This would prove to be 21-year-old Sumino's final kill, for he would perish in combat with yet more P-38s on 6 June. With the monsoon season fast approaching, the Japanese pilots felt that the weather that day would not be suitable for flying. To pass the time, Lt Sumino and Capt Miyabe were enjoying a game of 'Go' in the pilots' ready hut at Meiktila East airfield. Sumino was losing, and said, 'I wish the enemy would show up so that we could postpone this match'. Minutes later his call was answered by the news that 20 P-38s were approaching.

Miyabe and Sumino dashed for their Ki-43s and took off. Because the JAAF had detected the incoming raid in good time, the 64th Sentai was able to ambush the raiders from above. Miyabe saw a Ki-43 chasing a P-38 that was streaming fuel, but another Lightning was closing from dead astern. 'Look out behind! Enemy!', Miyabe called repeatedly over his radio, but the Ki-43 fell apart before his eyes when the P-38 opened fire. And although a parachute deployed, the pilot hung limply beneath it, having been mortally wounded prior to baling out. It was Sumino.

By the time of his death, Lt Sumino had been credited with 27 aerial victories, making him the 64th Sentai's ranking ace. He was described as being foolishly bold, his wingman, Cpl Itsuo Niwa, recalling that, 'Lt Sumino was an aggressive pilot who would never stop attacking even if he was in danger from an enemy aircraft behind him'. Exhausted following nine months of constant combat, the 64th Sentai was withdrawn to Saigon, in Indochina, the very next day.

P-38s also tangled with the 50th Sentai on 6 June, and 16-kill ace Sgt Tomesaku Igarashi claimed one shot down over Arakan Yomas after chasing several fighters from Meiktila. Having expended his ammunition, he then rammed the rudder of a second P-38 with the propeller of his Ki-43 and shot at the pilot when he baled out. Igarashi claimed his 16th, and last, kill on 17 June when he downed a twin-engined aircraft whilst leading a patrol over Imphal. His element was then bounced by 20+ Spitfires and Igarashi was duly shot down over Bishenpur and killed.

Despite the onset of the monsoon season, Allied forces continued to take the fight to the Japanese, unlike in previous years. With the 64th recuperating, the 50th and 204th Sentais were kept busy, attacking Imphal on 8 and 17 June and claiming six victories. On 7 July the 50th claimed 39 aircraft destroyed on the ground during a strafing attack, and 12 more were shot down two days later by both sentais for the loss of three Hayabusas. Finally, on 29 July a further six victories (including four of the first P-47s seen in Burma) were claimed over Myitkyina.

On 2 August, the 64th Sentai returned to Burma with new Ki-43 Model IIIs, which were 30 mph faster than the Model IIs. That was not all, as Cpl Masahiro Ikeda recalled;

'A shorter take-off run was one of the Model III's benefits. It could also maintain full throttle combat power for 40 minutes. If I'd done that for only 30 minutes with the Model II, I'd have had an earful from the mechanics. The Model II just couldn't handle that kind of load. Pitted against the Ki-44 and new Ki-84, the Model III made the best start.'

The 50th Sentai withdrew to Saigon to convert to the Ki-84 once the 64th was back in Burma, and the 204th was withdrawn to Thailand and then posted to the Philippines in October. The 64th would now be the sole operator of the Ki-43 in-theatre through to the fall of Rangoon, and the end of the war in Burma, in May 1945.

Amongst the pilots to enjoy early success with the new Ki-43-III was future ace Sgt Toshimi Ikezawa, who, at the end of August, downed a C-47 as it neared its drop zone west of Salween. He was flying alone at the time, having disobeyed orders by leaving his formation, as he recalled;

'I'd gained confidence in air combat while training in Saigon under Capt Miyabe. Back in Burma, I was determined to leave the formation once combat presented itself. Half of my classmates had been killed while flying in formations before the Imphal operation. New pilots were under strict orders never to leave formations, so they didn't get a chance to shoot down a single enemy aircraft. I thought it was ridiculous that I could be killed without scoring any aerial victories.

During the 1944 monsoon season, Capt Nakamura and other pilots from the 64th Sentai's 1st Chutai went to Thailand to instruct Thai Air Force pilots converting onto the Ki-43. Note the Thai elephant marking on the tail. The Thai officers are wearing their USAAF-inspired uniforms in this photograph (*64th Sentai Association*)

64th Sentai pilots selected to attack the Huitongqiao bridge are pictured at Meiktila airfield on 17 August 1944. They are, front row (from left to right), Sgt Maj Fujikawa, Capt Nakamura, Sentai CO Maj Toyoki Eto, Col Kuwazuka, unknown officer, Capt Kitazato and Sgt Maj Kato. And second row (left to right), Sgt Okada, Cpl Yamazaki and Sgts Yamamoto, Ikezawa, Ishida and Nakao. Ikezawa shot down a C-47 of the 27th TCS west of the River Salween during the Huitongqiao bridge mission (*64th Sentai Association*)

'The chutai leader was furious with me because I'd broken away from the formation, even though I had shot down an enemy aircraft. He was a bit less angry the second time I did this and completely silent the third time because I'd scored a victory on each occasion.'

The third Burmese 'Shooting Season' began in earnest in early October, and the first victory claimed by the 64th during this month came on the 5th when a single Beaufighter of No 177 Sqn made a low-level attack on Meiktila airfield. The Ki-43s of Capt Saburo Nakamura, Sgts Nakao and Ikezawa and Cpl Toshimi Ikeda were immediately scrambled, and ace Nakamura was eventually able to shoot the lone Beaufighter down after pursuing it at low level for more than 20 minutes.

The following day three Ki-43s were again ordered to scramble from Meiktila when 12 B-25s attacked the base. At the time of the raid Capt Nakamura had been lecturing his pilots on how to attack bombers, and he quickly put his words into practice when he dived at the B-25s head-on. Sgt Ikezawa quickly shot one down, as did Nakamura, but the latter's Ki-43 disintegrated when it was hit by the bombers' defensive fire during his next head-on pass. Although the ace's parachute opened, he was found to be dead when rescuers reached him – he had been shot through the forehead by a B-25 gunner.

Fellow ace Ikezawa recalled how Nakamura used to tell the members of his chutai, 'I'll never be killed by an enemy fighter. If I die, it'll be while attacking a bomber, or by anti-aircraft fire'. Capt Saburo Nakamura was credited with 20 aerial victories, and was posthumously awarded an individual citation and promoted two ranks. The 64th Sentai was losing its old hands one by one.

Although still routinely encountering Allied fighters and bombers as they targeted JAAF airfields and strategic targets in Rangoon, the 64th now found itself primarily flying ground support missions. The unit claimed some increasingly rare aerial kills on 5 November when a Spitfire and four RAF Dakotas were shot down near Imphal and Kalemyo, respectively. The following day, Sgt Ikezawa spotted a Mosquito flying away from Meiktila North. Noticing that one of its engines had been damaged by anti-aircraft fire, he gave chase and shot it down.

By early December, the 64th Sentai's Meiktila base was becoming a regular target for RAF fighter-bombers, but they rarely found any 'Oscars' to attack. 'Our Ki-43s were never caught on the ground', sentai operations officer Capt Teruo Aizawa boasted to the author. 'We stationed eight or ten mechanics at all the frontline airfields regularly frequented by our Ki-43s. We knew that the Allies would bomb the bases that our fighters took off from, so we would signal the returning pilots to fly to another airfield after these attacks.'

As 1944 drew to a close, most of the aerial combat in Burma was now being performed by the Ki-84-equipped 50th Sentai. 64th Sentai pilot Cpl Masahiro Ikeda told the author that his unit was also anxious to receive Hayates;

'We all had our hopes pinned on the Ki-84, but our new sentai commander, Maj Toyoki Eto, had told us we'd have to keep on using the Ki-43-IIIs, since problems were being experienced with the Hayate's engine. The Ki-43 was a highly manoeuvrable fighter, and very reliable, but we wanted a faster one that could get us into action and out of trouble quickly. The slower Ki-43 was always at the mercy of the faster enemy aircraft, because we couldn't get away quickly enough.'

Ironically, the 64th Sentai had been offered the new fighter before the 50th, as Sgt Ikezawa explained;

'I heard that Maj Eto had refused delivery of the Ki-84. The fighter had the speed to really scoot away if Spitfires attacked from above. A Hayate pilot would simply drop the nose and be off in a flash. They couldn't avoid an attack if it came from above, however, because of the Ki-84's poor rate of turn. This meant that the Hayates would routinely head for home while we were left to dogfight with the Spitfires. 50th Sentai pilots became notorious for firing a few cannon bursts at the enemy and then fleeing the scene. I think we owe our survival to the Ki-43, as the Ki-84 would have left you in a mighty tight spot if you were attacked from above by P-51s.'

From October to December 1944, 17 Ki-43s and one Ki-84 had been shot down in air combat, but JAAF fighters destroyed seven C-47s, five Liberators, two Spitfires, two Beaufighters, two Mosquitoes, two F4Us, two B-29s, one F6F, one P-38 and one B-25 during the same period – figures confirmed by Allied records.

The 64th carried out a series of Ta Dan bombing raids on Allied airfields in early January, and on the 9th, sentai CO Maj Toyoki Eto was forced to crash-land his Ki-43 after being shot up by a Spitfire during an attack on Akyab. He had claimed an RAF fighter moments earlier for his 12th kill.

Three days later, more Allied transports were destroyed in the air and on the ground at Onbauk airstrip, when RAF Dakotas were caught unloading supplies by 17 Ki-43s. No 435 Sqn admitted the

64th Sentai/1st Chutai pilots stand in front of a well used Ki-43-II pictured at Mingaladon in late 1944. They are (from left to right) Cpls Yamaguchi, Okamura and Masahiro Ikeda, Sgt Maj Fujikawa, Lt Imanishi and Sgt Kuramoto (*64th Sentai Association*)

loss of two aircraft in the air and two on the ground, plus one damaged. A UC-64 Norseman of the 1st ACG was riddled with shells while attempting to take off and two Stinson O-49A Vigilants from the same group were also lost.

At dusk on 11 February, 12 Ki-43s attacked the Allied fleet blockading Ramree Island with 250-kg bombs. They approached the target area out of the sun at 6500 ft, and saw many destroyers, submarine chasers and gunboats. Anti-aircraft gunners opened up as the Ki-43 pilots selected their targets. Sgt Ikezawa explained what happened next;

'I spotted a ship underway, so I separated from our formation. The sentai commander seemed to be taking us through an intense anti-aircraft barrage, so my wingman, Sgt Ikeda, joined me. We pulled off a surprise attack on the vessel, dropping our bombs from a height of about 650 ft without any anti-aircraft fire. I'm not sure if our bombs actually hit the ship. I was approaching the target beside Ikeda in a shallow dive. My Ki-43 was blown upwards by the shock wave of my bombs as I broke away at very low altitude. I glanced behind and saw two columns of smoke rising from the ship.'

The destroyer HMS *Pathfinder* was so badly damaged that it was subsequently scrapped. The Japanese evacuation of Ramree failed nevertheless, as only four small boats were able to break through the Allied blockade.

Missions such as this were now the norm for the 64th Sentai, as Sgt Ikezawa recalled;

'We were now almost exclusively flying ground attack sorties. After three strafing passes, the Spitfires would always show up overhead. Our altitude for these missions was about 3000 ft. The Spitfires would fly in at 5000-6000 ft. When they dived on us, we'd try to avoid them, but skilled enemy pilots such as flight leaders would pull out of their dives when they realised that they could not catch us. New pilots, perhaps the wingmen, would dive straight down on us, leaving them vulnerable in a turning fight. Indeed, if a Spitfire pilot tried to turn away, we'd have a chance to catch him. If he dived away, however, we'd couldn't stay with him.

'The Spitfire was an excellent fighter with a similar turning ability to the Ki-43. Its turning radius was actually wider, but much faster, so in the end its turning ability was the same as ours. What often saved us was the Spitfire's short operational range. If we could coax them down to lower altitudes, they'd eventually have to give up and go home.'

In late January British armoured spearheads advanced south into Burma as the Japanese Army retreated. On the 26th 14 Ki-43s of the 64th Sentai took off from Mingaladon in an attempt to blunt the Allied offensive. However, shortly after departing the base they were bounced by four USAAF P-47s, and future sentai CO Maj Hideo Miyabe claimed one damaged. Sgt Ikezawa then spotted another Thunderbolt over the airfield;

'At first, we mistook it for a twin-engined aircraft – the bombs under its wings looked like engines. When it turned out to be a P-47, I approached it with my wingman, Ikeda. The fighter turned to face us and then dived beneath us. If I'd also been in a P-47 I wouldn't have been able to attack him, but the Ki-43 could quickly stall turn, and we caught him easily. A burst from my guns sent him spinning into the ground. He must have been a novice pilot. If he'd just dived away at the start I wouldn't have been able to catch him.'

That evening British armoured forces overran Meiktila airfield – formerly the 64th Sentai's home in Burma.

Two Ki-43s were lost in air combat during February, but in return the 'Oscar' pilots accounted for two P-47s and one L-5 – losses corroborated by Allied records. In March, the JAAF's 5th Air Division forbade its fighter pilots from engaging enemy aircraft. The reason was simple, as Sgt Ikezawa explained;

'We were running out of aircraft. Of course, we were always short of supplies from Japan, like spark plugs. We had to use refurbished ones. We flew aircraft in that condition, with engines that might cut out every couple of minutes. That was why we were forbidden to engage enemy formations. This didn't really offer us much relief as we still had orders to attack lone enemy aircraft.'

Isolated aerial clashes occurred throughout April, however, and a No 17 Sqn Spitfire was claimed on the 24th by Taiwanese pilot Sgt Shotaro Konishi. This proved to be the 64th Sentai's last victory in Burma, and it is confirmed by Allied records.

After the 26th Indian Division captured Rangoon on 1 May, 64th Sentai Ki-43s dropped medical supplies to the Japanese troops who had retreated into the jungle on the Burmese-Thai border. At this time the unit was based at Takhli airfield, 90 miles north of Bangkok. Chiang Mai, Lampang and Nakhon Sawan were used as advanced airfields.

At dawn on 29 May, nine Ki-43s flew from Nakhon Sawan to Takhli. They had completed the unit's last air supply mission in the border area and were heading home when they sighted a Liberator III of No 358 Sqn dropping supplies to insurgent forces. Sgt Toshimi Ikezawa recalled that the bomber proved easy meat for the Ki-43 pilots;

'Flying over Thailand in groups of about ten aircraft, we'd often catch B-24s dropping personnel into the jungle by parachute. We'd line up astern of the bombers to make our attacks by the book, usually with two or three passes. Once, I got hit in the elevator while attacking from behind. Fellow ace WO Kosuke Tsubone said he was sure I was going to be shot down during the 29 May attack!'

This Liberator was the 64th Sentai's final victory, and its loss is confirmed by Allied records.

On 9 July, the unit's ten Ki-43s moved to Vinh airfield, in Indochina. Two days later the base was attacked by P-51s, and Sgts Ikezawa and Ikeda, who were known as the 'Ike-Ike element', scrambled and tried to chase one of the USAAF fighters, but it was too fast for them. When they abandoned the pursuit another P-51 appeared and then dived away. Ikeda fired at it but the result was inconclusive. He later recalled;

'I'm sure I got that P-51 but it was an unconfirmed victory. I attacked another coming from below, and Kato was there too. There was a further P-51 but I didn't see it, as I was focusing on what was happening below. We must have clipped each other some time during the battle, because

This rare photograph shows Capt Hideo Miyabe at the controls of his personal Ki-43-III in late 1944. The final production variant of the Hayabusa, the fighter made its frontline debut with the 64th Sentai over Burma in October 1944. The two bands around the fighter's fuselage immediately behind the cockpit denote that this 'Oscar' was assigned to the hikotai leader (*Hideo Miyabe*)

after I landed I found that half my rudder was missing – not due to an attack but a collision. That pilot must've been surprised, too. I didn't realise there had been a collision so I continued the attack. I was over unfamiliar territory though, so I eventually returned to base. The groundcrew from Taiwan said it was the first time they'd seen Japanese fighters pursuing enemy aircraft. Previously in Taiwan, Japanese pilots would simply run away when enemy aircraft were encountered.'

On 24 July the 64th Sentai flew to Sungai Petani airfield, in Malaya, to join the attack on an Allied aircraft carrier task force sighted off Phuket, but this operation was ultimately abandoned. The unit then transferred to Kurakore airfield, in Cambodia. On 15 August, Sgt Ikeda was part of a detachment of four Ki-43s assigned to escort a convoy, but the aircraft were ordered to return to base. Japan had surrendered.

In late August two dark-coloured Dakotas landed at Kurakore with an escort of Spitfires. In front of his assembled pilots and groundcrew, Maj Miyabe talked to the British officers who had arrived in the aircraft. It had been rumoured that Japanese pilots responsible for the death of substantial numbers of Allied aircrew would be executed. Sgt Satoshi Kawazumi had hidden a pistol in the pocket of his flying suit, and he planned to use it if the rumour turned out to be true. Sgts Ikezawa and Ikeda watched sullenly as the discussions continued. When asked how many Allied aircraft he had shot down, Miyabe replied, 'Ten, more or less'. The answer was greeted with some surprise, and the 26-year-old CO felt it might have been more prudent to have given a figure of two or three. But the matter was resolved, the Japanese were disarmed and the Dakotas departed.

During several more visits the pilots of both sides were able to re-live some of their encounters. When an RAF pilot showed Miyabe camera-gun film of a Ki-43 twisting to avoid a burst of gunfire, he noted the slanting white lines painted on the wings of the Japanese fighter, which distinguished it as that of a sentai commander.

Later, Miyabe called for a volunteer to fly with a Spitfire. All of his pilots raised their hands, but he selected the oldest, ten-kill ace WO Kosuke Tsubone. A Spitfire and a Ki-43 duly took off for a 20-minute flying display over Kurakore. Finally, both fighters flew so low over the runway that their slipstreams raised clouds of dust. Then the former enemies climbed to 1000 m, with Tsubone keeping close to the Spitfire.

Masahiro Ikeda told the author, 'I thought the Spitfire pilot had been making allowances for the Ki-43'.

The 64th Sentai's main force of 280 men returned to Japan on 4 May 1946. After a speech by Miyabe, they sang 'Kato Hayabusa Sento-Tai', one of the most popular Japanese military songs. Then the unit was disbanded. The men were given a bag of rice, some ration coupons and a train ticket home. That was their reward for four years of bitter fighting.

Maj Miyabe (far right) became the 64th Sentai's final commander in April 1945 when 12-kill ace Maj Toyoki Eto was posted back to Japan. Miyabe fostered teamwork, shunned publicity and would not even acknowledge his own aerial victories (at least ten) (*Hideo Miyabe*)

1
Ki-43-I of the 64th Sentai, flown by Maj Tateo Kato, Palembang, Sumatra, February 1942

2
Ki-43-I of the 64th Sentai/2nd Chutai, flown by Capt Masuzo Ohtani, Chiang Mai, Thailand, March 1942

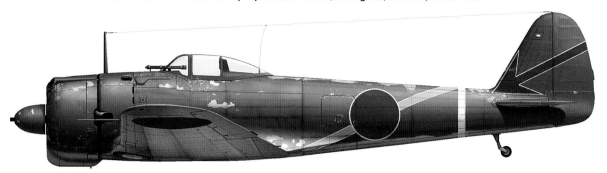

3
Ki-43-I of the 64th Sentai/2nd Chutai, flown by Lt Saburo Nakamura, Mingaladon, Burma, early December 1942

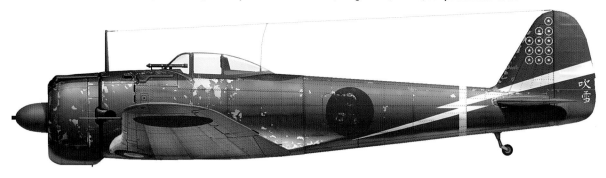

4
Ki-43-I of the 50th Sentai/3rd Chutai, flown by Sgt Satoshi Anabuki and Lt Shigeru Nakazaki, Toungoo, Burma, January 1943

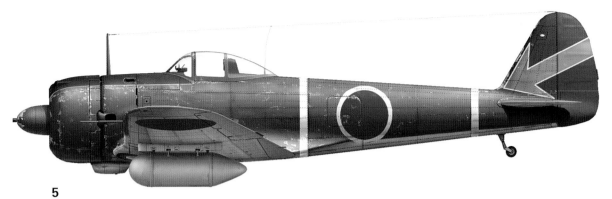

5
Ki-43-II of the 64th Sentai, flown by Capt Yasuhiko Kuroe, Toungoo, Burma, March 1943

6
Ki-43-II of the 50th Sentai/2nd Chutai, flown by Capt Masao Miyamaru, Toungoo, Burma, May 1943

7
Ki-43-II of the 64th Sentai/2nd Chutai, flown by Sgt Miyoshi Watanabe, Toungoo, Burma, March-April 1943

8
Ki-43-II of the 64th Sentai/3rd Chutai, flown by Lt Yohei Hinoki, Mingaladon, Burma, November 1943

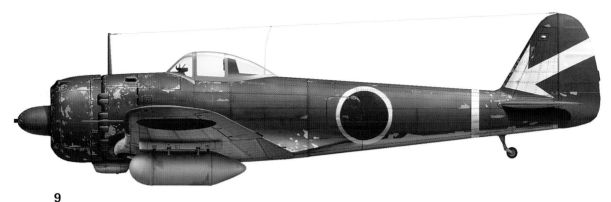

9
Ki-43-III of the 64th Sentai/1st Chutai, flown by Sgt Toshimi Ikezawa, Meiktila, Burma, November 1944

10
Ki-43-III of the 64th Sentai, flown by Maj Hideo Miyabe, Kurakore, Indochina, May 1945

11
Ki-43-I of the 24th Sentai/2nd Chutai, Canton, China, July 1942

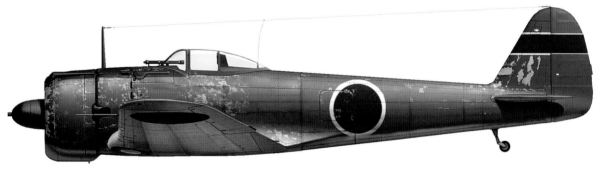

12
Ki-43-I of the 10th Dokuritsu Hiko Chutai (10th Independent Flying Chutai), Canton, China, August 1942

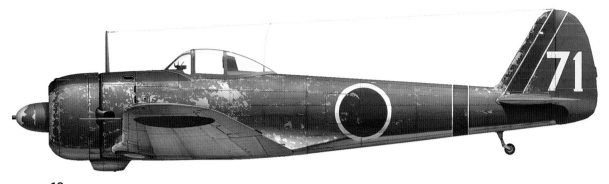

13
Ki-43-II of the 25th Sentai/2nd Chutai, flown by Capt Nakakazu Ozaki, Hankow, China, summer 1943

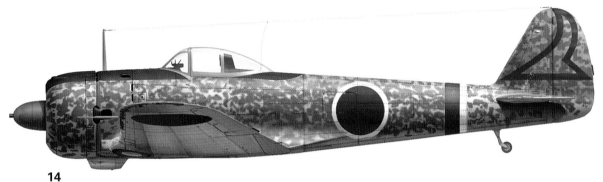

14
Ki-43-II of the 33rd Sentai/2nd Chutai, flown by Capt Kiyoshi Namai, Hanoi, Indochina, September 1943

15
Ki-43-II of the 25th Sentai/2nd Chutai, flown by Sgt Maj Kyushiro Ohtake, Hankow, China, December 1943

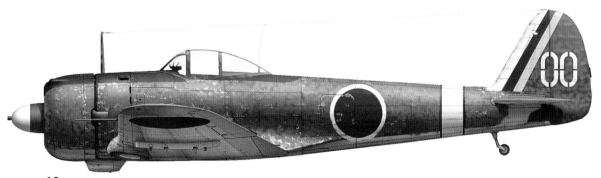

16
Ki-43-II of the 25th Sentai, flown by Maj Toshio Sakagawa, Hankow, late 1943

17
Ki-43-II of the 25th Sentai/2nd Chutai, flown by Sgt Maj Iwataro Hazawa, Hankow, China, spring 1944

18
Ki-43-II of the 25th Sentai/3rd Chutai flown by Capt Keisaku Motohashi, Hankow, China, spring 1944

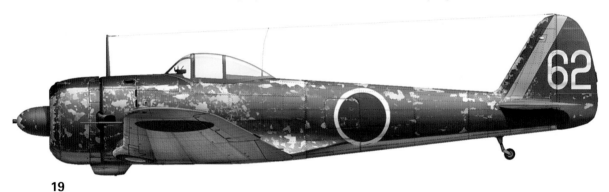

19
Ki-43-II of the 25th Sentai/2nd Chutai, flown by Cpl Haruyuki Todai, Hankow, China, spring 1944

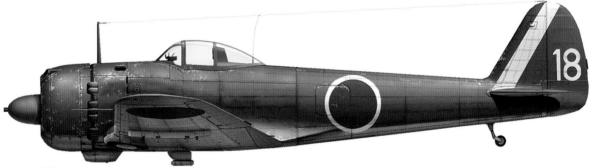

20
Ki-43-III of the 25th Sentai/1st Chutai, flown by Sgt Goro Miyamoto, Hengyang, China, November 1944

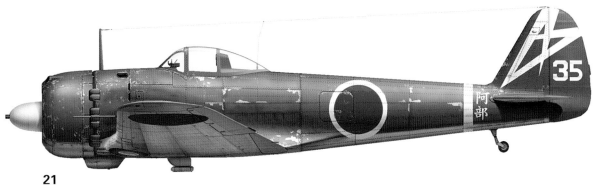

21
Ki-43-III of the 48th Sentai/1st Chutai, flown by Sgt Sou Okabe, Nanking, China, August 1945

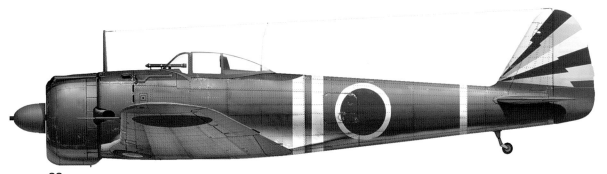

22
Ki-43-I of the 11th Sentai, flown by Maj Katsuji Sugiura, Mingaladon, Burma, November 1942

23
Ki-43-I of the 1st Sentai/1st Chutai, Akeno Fighter School, Japan, July 1942

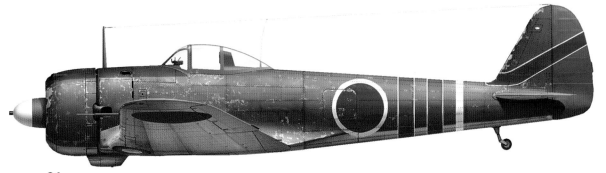

24
Ki-43-II of the 59th Sentai/2nd Chutai, flown by Capt Shigeo Nango, But, New Guinea, September 1943

25
Ki-43-II of the 59th Sentai/3rd Chutai, flown by Sgt Maj Tomio Hirohata, But, New Guinea, October 1943

26
Ki-43-II of the 63rd Sentai/1st Chutai, Wewak, New Guinea, early 1944

27
Ki-43-II of the 248th Sentai/2nd Chutai, Hollandia, New Guinea, March 1944

28
Ki-43-II of the 77th Sentai/2nd Chutai, flown by Capt Yoshihide Matsuo, Wewak, New Guinea, June 1944

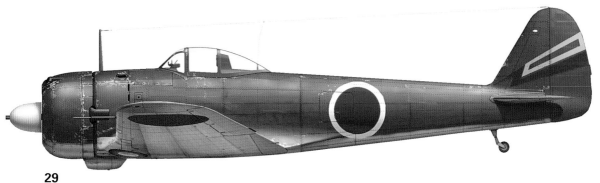

29
Ki-43-II of the 20th Sentai/1st Chutai, Hsiaochiang, Formosa, October 1944

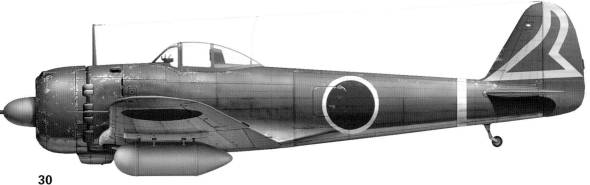

30
Ki-43-III of the 33rd Sentai/3rd Chutai, flown by Lt Hitoshi Yamamoto, Legaspi, Luzon, the Philippines, November 1944

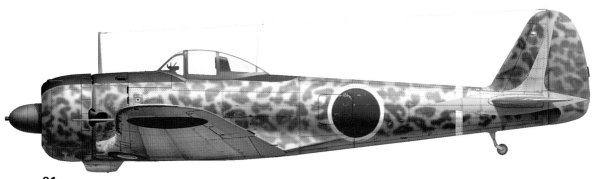

31
Ki-43-II of the 54th Sentai/3rd Chutai, flown by WO Akira Sugimoto, Fabrica, Negros Island, the Philippines, January 1945

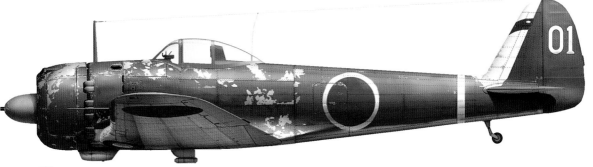

32
Ki-43-III of the 204th Sentai, flown by Capt Hiroshi Murakami, Hualien, Formosa, July 1945

CHINA FIGHTING

Although the Ki-43 had been seen in Chinese skies just prior to the commencement of the Greater East Asian War, both the 59th and 64th Sentais had been posted south to fight over Malaya by 7 December 1941. The Hayabusa would be absent from the China front until June 1942, leaving Ki-27s of the 10th Independent Flying Chutai and 24th, 33rd and 54th Sentais to periodically battle with AVG P-40Bs.

Although the 'Nates' were flown by veteran fighter pilots, the aircraft had trouble catching the appreciably faster Curtiss fighter. So, it was with great relief that the 10th Independent Flying Chutai switched to the Ki-43-I at Akeno in May-June 1942. The 24th Sentai (a battle-hardened unit which had fought in the Nomonhan Incident against the USSR in 1939) followed suit the following month, arriving in China on 23 July. Both units would be based at Canton throughout the summer of 1942, and they would regularly clash with the AVG, and the China Air Task Force (CATF) that succeeded it in July of that year.

The 10th Independent Flying Chutai flew its first missions alongside the Ki-27s of the 54th Sentai on 3 and 4 July, when they attacked the CATF airfield at Hengyang. The first victories claimed by the 'Oscar' in China came on 30 July, when 27 Ki-43s from the 24th Sentai and 12 from the 10th Independent Flying Chutai attacked Hengyang once again. Only ten CATF P-40s rose to intercept the 'Oscars', with JAAF pilots later reporting that they seemed anxious to avoid fighting a pitched battle with the Japanese, who were keen to engage in dogfights. The P-40 pilots preferred their usual hit and run tactics.

Frustrated, the 24th Sentai claimed to have shot one Warhawk down, plus a probable, for no loss, but the 10th Independent Flying Chutai reported two aerial victories and another two enemy aircraft destroyed on the ground. One Ki-43 was missing and another two were damaged. Conversely, from the USAAF's perspective, the first clash between Ki-43s and CATF P-40s had ended with the latter claiming the destruction of three 'Oscars', plus one probable, for no loss.

The 24th Sentai returned the next morning to claim four P-40s shot down and another as a probable, but it in turn lost three Ki-43s and their pilots over Hengyang. The surviving crews had been shocked to see their much-vaunted new fighters disintegrating in mid-air one by one as they attempted to pull out of dives. Two pilots were so rattled that they damaged their undercarriages upon returning to Canton. The CATF was credited with six confirmed victories without loss. The Ki-43 pilots had lost their first two duels with the P-40s in China.

Although of indifferent quality, this rare photograph shows Ki-43-Is from the 24th Sentai being run up at Canton in July 1942. On the last day of that month, pilots from the unit gave the Hayabusa its combat debut in China when they engaged CATF P-40s over Hengyang *(Yasuho Izawa)*

Despite reservations over the structural integrity of the 'Oscar', both units continued to take the fight to the CATF in coming months during regular attacks on airfields at Hengyang, Lingling and Kweilin. With relatively few USAAF aircraft in theatre, Ki-43 pilots found it hard to build up big scores in China, and by the time the 24th Sentai left Canton for Sumatra in September 1942, it had claimed just 17 kills and six probables for the loss of five pilots. The only confirmed kill credited to an ace flying with the unit during this time was awarded to WO Mitsuo Ogura, who downed a P-40 for the first of his 16 victories.

The 24th was replaced at Canton by the 33rd Sentai, which had swapped its Ki-27s for Ki-43-Is. The unit claimed two B-25s over Hong Kong on 25 October and a P-40 three days later.

In early November the 10th Independent Flying Chutai became the 25th Sentai when it received sufficient Ki-43-Is to form a second chutai – a third would be created in the spring. Its first CO was Maj Toshio Sakagawa, who was a highly experienced fighter pilot that had seen combat in the final stage of the Nomonhan Incident as a chutai leader with the 24th Sentai in 1939. He had taken command of the 47th Independent Flying Chutai, which was equipped with nine pre-production Ki-44 Type 2 interceptors from the JAAF Flight Test Centre, in December 1941. Capt Yasuhiko Kuroe was one of his pilots, and they had fought together in Malaya and Burma until April 1942 (see chapter two), when Kuroe was transferred to the 64th Sentai as 3rd Chutai leader and Sakagawa returned to Japan to report the results of the Ki-44 deployment. In November 1942 he was sent to China as CO of the 25th Sentai.

Sakagawa would score heavily in China, leading his sentai by example until he was eventually posted back to the Akeno Fighter School in July 1944. By then his tally stood at 15 victories, and the 25th had easily become the leading fighter unit in-theatre, boasting nine aces in total.

A handful of victories were claimed over southern China in November and December 1942, prior to the units moving to Wuchang, in central China, in January 1943. Again, victories were few and far between, and both sides made inflated claims. However, it was obvious that JAAF losses in both fighters and bombers at that time greatly exceeded those of the CATF. The JAAF claims were optimistic in mission after mission, but it was clear that the real victor was the CATF.

In March the USAAF's Fourteenth Air Force was formed to take control of growing American air assets in China from the CATF. Still, the primary fighter encountered by the JAAF was the P-40, and a number were claimed to have been shot down in late April in a series of raids on Lingling, Yunnan and Kunming. However, the following month saw a series of losses inflicted on both sentais, with five pilots being killed on 2 May alone after being chased back from Lingling. On a more positive note, the 33rd claimed seven more kills before the month was out, the sentai continuing to fly missions whilst converting to the Ki-43-II.

Things improved for both units in June, with 49 kills being claimed by month end for the loss of five Ki-43s (three on the 14th from the 33rd) and two pilots killed. Most victories fell to the 33rd, as the 25th Sentai had returned to Japan on 15 June to exchange its Ki-43-Is for Model IIs.

It was planned that the unit would be back in China in time for it to participate in the JAAF's 'Summer Air Operation', which began on 23

24th Sentai ace WO Mitsuo Ogura claimed the first of his 16 kills over China. The rest of his victories came in New Guinea and the Philippines *(Yasuho Izawa)*

The 25th Sentai's first commander was Maj Toshio Sakagawa, who was transferred in to lead the new unit from the Dokuhi 47th (47th Independent Flying) Chutai. Whilst serving as a chutai leader with the 47th, one of Sakagawa's pilots had been future ranking 59th Sentai ace Capt Yasuhiko Kuroe *(Yasuho Izawa)*

The 25th Sentai exchanged its Ki-43-Is for Model IIs in June 1943. The white stripe on the fin of this early-build Model II seen at Hankow indicates that it belonged to the 1st Chutai *(Yasuho Izawa)*

July with repeat attacks on USAAF bases by Ki-48s and Ki-21s, escorted by the 25th Sentai. US fighter tactics proved highly effective, however. Forewarned of the approaching JAAF formations, the P-40 pilots waited at higher altitude and dived at high speed through the escorting Ki-43s and decimated the lightly protected bombers with their six 0.50-in machine guns. And like the JAAF fighter pilots, their P-40 counterparts overclaimed in respect to the number of aircraft that they had shot down.

Ki-43 units participated in a series of escort missions between 23 and 31 July, claiming 19 kills for the loss of 11 pilots. Following this all out effort, the JAAF scaled back operations until Kweilin was bombed on 20 August. The 33rd claimed three kills for one loss, but then had four pilots killed over Hengyang the following day. Having completed their mission, the 25th and 33rd Sentais were preparing to land at Hankow when they were bounced by P-40s that had shadowed them back to their base.

Two hours later, the Fourteenth Air Force sent B-24s to attack the JAAF airfield in Hankow as the USAAF went on the offensive. Senior American officers in China felt that the heavy bombers of the 308th BG could strike targets in daylight despite the strong Japanese fighter presence. Indeed, the USAAF had still to lose a B-24 in this theatre. Realising that it was only a matter of time before Liberators started appearing over key targets in China on a regular basis, the 25th and 33rd Sentais received information from the 50th Sentai in Burma about the tactics the unit had employed so successfully against the heavily armed bombers over Rangoon. Pilots also received head-on attack training.

25th Sentai Ki-43s, led by Maj Sakagawa, took off from Hankow to intercept approaching bogies detected by the JAAF's 15th Air Surveillance Unit radar at Yochow. It had spotted 14 B-24Ds of the 374th and 375th BSs, led by Maj Bruce Beat. Having missed their rendezvous with their fighter escorts over Hengyang, the bombers were unprotected.

Thanks to the ample radar warning, the Ki-43 pilots were able to attack the bombers long before they reached the target. Sakagawa hit Beat's lead Liberator in his first head-on pass. The bomber went into a steep dive, and was followed by the rest of the formation, whose crews assumed Beat was leading them in avoiding action. The B-24 eventually burst into flames and the Ki-43 pilots saw two parachute canopies.

Without their leader, the remaining B-24s pressed on through a swarm of 'Oscars' towards the target – Hankow's harbour area. The bombers' gunners were shooting furiously, but the B-24s scattered one after the other in the face of determined attacks by the Ki-43s. A second Liberator from the 375th crash-landed on a sandbar after being chased by several Ki-43s. Three crewmembers were killed, but the others were rescued by Chinese guerrillas, who had to fight their way through a force of Japanese troops to reach them.

Another B-24 made an emergency landing at Lingling fighter airfield, having been badly shot up. The remaining ten bombers limped back to their base at Kweilin, with nine of them having been damaged to varying degrees.

A Ki-43-II of the 33rd Sentai's 2nd Chutai sits in the open at Canton in the late summer of 1943. Note the sentai's distinctive insignia on the tail of the Hayabusa. Very few photos of 33rd Sentai 'Oscars' have come to light *(Yasuho Izawa)*

It was the first defeat suffered by the B-24 force in China. Yet despite losing two aircraft, bomber gunners filed claims for 57 fighters shot down and 13 probably destroyed! The 25th Sentai did no lose a single pilot!

On the 23rd, Ki-43s of the 25th and 33rd Sentais escorted Ki-21s of the 58th Sentai to the Kuomintang capital of Chongquing. The Chinese early warning set up (both radar and ground observers) was as effective as usual, and eight Republic P-43s, ten P-40s and eleven Vultee P-66s of the CAF's 4th Air Battalion took off to lay an ambush.

The air battle began long before the raiding force reached its target. The CAF claimed two Ki-21s and, indeed, one of the 58th Sentai's machines failed to return. But the 25th Sentai claimed two P-43s and three probables, plus a P-40 and another unidentified fighter. According to records, one P-40 or P-43 pilot was killed and another baled out. Two P-66s were also missing. The 33rd Sentai claimed no aerial victories and all of its Ki-43s returned home safely.

The next day, 14 B-24s of the 308th BG's 373rd and 425th BSs were prepared for another attack on Hankow – the 374th and 375th BSs had not yet recovered from their mauling on the 20th. Close escort took the form of 16 P-40s, with eight P-38s flying top cover. At the same time, six B-25s of the 11th BS were to bomb Wuchang airfield on the opposite shore to Hankow. In the event, seven B-24s of the 373rd were frustrated by bad weather and turned back, leaving the 425th to attack the target.

A JAAF air surveillance post 63 miles south-southeast of Hankow provided a warning to the 25th and 33rd Sentais that B-24s were inbound, and the units scrambled a number of fighters. But the latter mistakenly attacked Wuchang ten minutes after the B-25s, and as they made a wide turn for home, the Ki-43s pounced. By then Col Bruce Holloway had assigned ten P-40s to another B-25 force that was making a low-level attack on the airfield, leaving only six P-40s to protect the heavy bombers from the 40 Ki-43s now climbing towards them. In a post-war interview, 33rd Sentai veteran Sumio Fujisaki said;

'We were ordered never to attack bombers from behind. It was very difficult. We made a head-on pass at the B-25s, which were fast and agile, then we concentrated on the slower B-24s.'

Six P-40s led by Capt Arthur Cruikshank fought bravely against overwhelming odds, and they managed to down 33rd Sentai pilot Sgt Yukiji Nogawa – he baled out, but later died in hospital. The P-40s then became involved in a dogfight with the remaining Ki-43s. Writing 49 years after the event, 425th BS veteran Lt Col Donald Kohsiek said, 'I can still visualise the lines of "Zeros" paralleling our course and peeling off one at a time to attack and then pass right over the top of us'.

Maj Akira Watanabe, leading the 33rd Sentai, attacked the lead B-24 in his first pass. His pilots were able to repeat this move three or four times in perfect order without any interference from the P-40s. Their first victim was the left-wing B-24 of A Flight. It started streaming a thin trail of smoke from its No 3 engine, before losing height and falling into a spin – three crew baled out. The second to go down was B Flight's left-wing B-24. Five crewmen bailed out. B Flight's right wing Liberator was then set on fire and six parachutes were seen, while the same flight's tail-end B-24 was riddled with shells and two engines were rendered useless. The pilot decided to bale out when none of his crew answered his call except for the upper turret gunner, who reported being out of ammunition.

B Flight's lead aircraft had taken 200 hits, which killed the tail gunner and seriously wounded four other crew members, but the crippled B-24 was able to make an emergency landing at Kweiling. The lead bomber of A Flight also sustained many hits, but it limped back to Hengyang advanced fighter base. Lt Col Kohsiek recalled, 'We went looking for those fighter pilots who had let us down so badly. I was going to kill them. I mean kill, I was so angry.' He did not know that fighter escort leader Col Holloway had spotted a Ki-43 attacking three surviving B-24s. He and his wingman shot it down 100 miles south of Wuchang. WO Hasumi Kono of the 25th Sentai was the third, and last, JAAF casualty of this combat – amongst those killed was 33rd Sentai CO Maj Watanabe.

Four of the seven B-24s that had attacked Wuchang had been shot down. The 308th BG had lost six bombers in two missions, resulting in two of its four squadrons being put out of operation for several weeks.

All Ki-43 sentais moved south in September, and on the 9th the 25th Sentai claimed two kills over Canton – one was credited to Maj Sakagawa.

As previously mentioned, the 308th BG's 373rd BS had not suffered at the hands of the Ki-43s, and on 31 August it had combined forces with the refitted 375th BS in an attack on Hanoi, in Indochina. The latter target, although well defended by anti-aircraft batteries, then lacked any JAAF fighter protection. A second raid was planned for 15 September, when the target was Haiphong, 63 miles east of Hanoi. Two days before the latter raid, the 25th Sentai and 33rd Sentai escorted Ki-21s of the 58th and 60th Sentais on a raid to Kunming. The fighter units claimed 18 victories for the loss of five bombers and a Hayabusa.

Lt Tameyoshi Kuroki was one of only three pilots to achieve ace status whilst flying with the 33rd Sentai. Serving exclusively with this unit from August 1938 (when it became a fighter sentai) until it disbanded at war's end, he claimed 16 victories in total. Kuroki downed three Soviet fighters during his first combat sortie on 5 September 1939 and claimed his final kill – an F6F Hellcat – whilst defending the Japanese home islands in February 1945 *(Yasuho Izawa)*

Lt Isamu Hosono had claimed 21 aerial victories with the 1st Sentai during the Nomonhan Incident, and he went on to claim a further five victories with the 25th Sentai between May 1943 and when he was killed in combat with P-40s over Suichuan on 6 October 1943 *(Yasuho Izawa)*

The Ki-43s had staged through Hanoi's Gia Lam airfield during this mission, and they were still at the base when the USAAF B-24s were detected approaching Haiphong on the 15th. Five B-24Ds of the 373rd BS, flying without fighter escort, were intercepted by 35 Ki-43s on the 15th. One of the pilots involved in this action was future 12-kill ace Capt Kiyoshi Namai of the 33rd Sentai, who recalled in a post-war interview;

'The B-24s had been detected by JAAF air surveillance posts on the border between China and Vietnam. We were accurately led to them by ground radio control.'

The intruders were attacked by 12 Ki-43s of the 25th Sentai's 2nd Chutai, led by future ace Lt Nakakazu Ozaki. The latter would become known as the 'B-24 killer' because six of his 19 victories were over heavy bombers. The best marksman in the 25th Sentai, his speciality was to attack Liberators from the side and front until he could actually hear the fire of his adversary's machine guns.

The Ki-43 pilots focused on the lead B-24, which spun into the sea. The remaining bombers scattered, and a second machine had its No 3 engine set on fire during the fighters' first pass. The other 'heavies' jettisoned their loads to make good their escape. Capt Namai remembered;

'We intercepted them with the full strength of our sentai. I led the 1st Chutai against three B-24s in formation. Our Ki-43s attacked them obliquely from the front in good order. We set one of them on fire, and the two survivors, trailing fuel or smoke, jettisoned their bombs and fled.'

A third B-24 dropped out of formation and was downed by Ki-43s and the fourth machine crashed near the Chinese border. Just one Liberator got back to base, where its gunners claimed to have shot down ten Ki-43s. However, the JAAF's sole casualty was Sgt Maj Chuzaburo Imai of the 25th Sentai. Later that same day, 12 Ki-43s of the 25th Sentai's 1st Chutai, led by future eight-kill ace Capt Takashi Tsuchiya, intercepted six B-25s of the 11th BS and 14 P-40s of the 23rd FG over Hankow. Lt Watanabe shot down the P-40 of 16th FS CO Lt Col Pike over Wuchang, the latter parachuting into captivity.

The 308th BG bombed Haiphong again on 1 October, escorted by 24 P-40s. All the B-24s returned safely, but three P-40s were lost and two Chinese pilots killed. Two Ki-43s were shot down and both pilots perished. Five days later, the 25th Sentai lost 21-kill Nomonhan Incident ace Lt Isamu Hosono, who had claimed five victories in China since joining the unit in May 1943. Bounced by P-40s during a bomber escort mission to Suichuan, and with his fighter trailing black smoke, Hosono chose to dive into a river from a height of 1600 ft when he realised he could not make it home. Becoming a PoW was forbidden to Japanese servicemen at that time, and Hosono's final act was reported in newspapers back home as being 'the best example of correct, courageous behaviour'.

The 33rd Sentai moved to the Burma front shortly after the JAAF's summer offensive ended on 6 October, by which point it had claimed 50 victories for the loss of 30 pilots since transitioning to the Ki-43 in May 1942.

During its summer operation, which lasted from 23 July to 6 October, the JAAF's 3rd Air Division in China claimed 113 aerial victories, but at a cost of 49 aircraft – 25 fighters, 14 bombers and one transport aircraft – and 130 aircrew. During the same period, the USAAF lost some 30 aircraft and 80-90 aircrew. The 25th Sentai was credited with 54 victories

Capt Nakakazu Ozaki, leader of the 25th Sentai's 2nd Chutai, was known as a 'B-24 killer', for among the 19 aerial victories credited to him were six Liberators. Between them, Ki-43 pilots of the 25th and 33rd Sentais shot down ten B-24s from the 308th BG within the space of just a month in August-September 1943 *(Yasuho Izawa)*

Eight-kill ace Capt Takashi Tsuchiya, leader of the 25th Sentai's 1st Chutai, took his unit into battle over Hankow against six B-25s of the 11th BS and 14 P-40s of the 23rd FG on 15 September 1943 while other sentai pilots tackled B-24s targeting Hanoi *(Yasuho Izawa)*

– 36 P-40s, eight B-24s and seven P-38s – at a cost of eight pilots lost. According to both JAAF and Allied records, the 25th Sentai had accounted for six B-24s, two P-40s, two P-43s, one P-38 and one P-66. This is ten short of total Allied fighter and bomber losses, so the 25th Sentai *actually* downed 15-20 aircraft during the 1943 summer operation.

Despite having suffered heavy losses to USAAF and CAF fighters, the JAAF considered the summer offensive a success because it resulted in the Fourteenth Air Force scaling back its activities in China. The real reason for this, however, was a reduction in the number of supply missions being flown over the Himalayas because of bad weather and the implementation of Operation *Tsujigiri* in northern Burma by the 50th Sentai .

Although struggling to keep aircraft serviceable, the USAAF continued to take the fight to the Japanese. On 29 October, for example, Chinese intelligence reported to the Fourteenth Air Force that Japanese supply vessels had assembled off Kiukang, in the Yangtze River. The next morning, eight P-38s of the 449th FS prepared to attack with 500-lb bombs, although they found 25th Sentai Ki-43s waiting for them. The P-38s were caught in a pincer movement by two groups of six 'Oscars' attacking from 'three o'clock' and 'nine o'clock high'. Four P-38s were shot down for the loss of one Ki-43.

The sentai next engaged the USAAF on 21 November when it escorted nine Ki-48s in a raid on the CAF base at Enshi. The 11th Air Battalion took off to defend the airfield, and it jumped the 21 JAAF machines from above and behind. The CAF pilots claimed four victories, but in the process lost three P-66s and their pilots. The 25th Sentai claimed eight victories, and all the Ki-43s and Ki-48s returned safety.

In early December, the Ki-43-II-equipped 11th Sentai was posted to Wuchang from Manchuria, but it would only stay in China for four months before returning to Japan to convert to the Ki-84 Hayate.

Late in the year fighting broke out at Changte, in Hunan Province, which saw CAF and Fourteenth Air Force units making repeated attacks on Japanese troops surrounding the city. On 3 December future 15-kill ace Sgt Maj Eiji Seino of the 25th Sentai engaged eight P-40s 19 miles northeast of Changte and claimed to have destroyed one and damaged another. Two P-40s of the 75th FS were indeed damaged, with both fighters force-landing and one being burnt out. Three days later, the 25th Sentai engaged P-40s of the China-America Composite Wing's 32nd FS over Changte. Two Warhawks were downed without loss.

On Christmas Eve, JAAF radar detected 29 B-24s of the 308th BG, escorted by three P-51As and 12 P-40s, on their way to attack Tien Ho airfield. The fighters were soon engaged by the 11th and 85th Sentais, operating under radio control from the ground. This left the B-24s unescorted, and as they advanced towards the target, the bombers were attacked by the 25th Sentai. A formation led by 'B-24 killer' Capt Ozaki singled out a Liberator from the 374th BS, causing its right landing gear to become unlocked and the bomber to then fall away in a spin. Ozaki and his men damaged five more B-24s before finally returning to base.

Two days later, he and his wingman intercepted more than 20 P-51As while escorting JAAF bombers sent to attack Suichuan airfield. Ozaki immediately rammed one of his opponents and then crashed to his death. Credited with 19 victories and inflicting damage on 12-14 B-24s, Ozaki

Noteworthy in this photograph of the Ki-43-II flown by 25th Sentai ace Capt Ozaki is the bullet hole visible in the leading edge of the left wing. This might have been the result of a head-on attack on a USAAF B-24. The fighter is also missing its left aileron. Ozaki was killed in combat on 27 December 1943 when he rammed a P-51A with his 'Oscar' over Suichuan *(Yasuho Izawa)*

was the 25th Sentai's joint leading ace (with Lt Moritsugu Kanai) in China in World War 2.

On 28 January 1944, the 25th Sentai received a special citation in recognition of it scoring 100 aerial victories. Of this total, 24 – seven B-24s, five P-38s, five P-40s, four P-66s and three P-43s – closely matched Allied loss records for the period between 2 November 1942 and 28 January 1944. The records also state that 23 aircraft – 12 P-40s, one P-43, two B-24s, seven P-38s and one P-66 – were downed during actions involving the sentai. On this basis, the unit's actual number of kills was nearer 30 to 40, and it lost 25 pilots in combat during the same period.

In February 1944, the JAAF's 3rd Air Division in China was re-allocated to 5th Air Force to provide air support for Japanese ground forces preparing for Operation *Ichi-Go* and the destruction of USAAF bases being prepared for strategic bombing attacks on the Japanese home islands. Amongst the pilots to see action that month was 11th Sentai ace Capt Hironojo Shishimoto, whose section fought P-38s, P-40s and P-51s on 12 February over Suichuan. The Ki-43 pilots claimed four fighters destroyed between them, but Sgt Maj Kenjiro Kurihara was killed.

Allied aircraft did their best to hamper the build up of Japanese forces for the offensive, and on 4 March the 25th Sentai's 3rd Chutai scrambled to intercept six P-38s from the 449th FS that were strafing river vessels near Kuikang. Three of them were downed when bounced by the Ki-43s.

Five days later, the CACW and Fourteenth Air Force made further attempts to disrupt Yangtze River traffic when 13 B-25s and 24 P-40s attacked the important harbour of Kuikiang. They were met by the 25th Sentai, as well as the Ki-44 equipped 9th Sentai. Pilots from the former unit claimed to have shot down two P-40s without loss – the CACW lost one Warhawk and its pilot, and three other P-40s and B-25s were damaged. On 10 March Nomonhan ace Lt Moritsugu Kanai claimed a P-38 destroyed over Anking for his first kill with the 25th Sentai in World War 2. By year-end he would be the unit's joint top-scoring ace in China.

In early April 1944, the newly re-equipped 48th Sentai was posted to Wuchang following its conversion from Ki-27s to Ki-43-IIs. This unit had been operating as a training sentai in Manchuria since July 1943, but it was now needed to help bolster JAAF ranks in preparation for *Ichi-Go*, which would be launched in late May.

Hankow was a key supply base for the offensive, and on 6 May the Fourteenth Air Force sent 40 fighters and bombers to attack it. Detected

25th Sentai pilots start the engines of their Ki-43-IIs at Hankow in the spring of 1944. The low walls of the revetments provided scant protection from air attacks by marauding Fourteenth Air Force bombers and fighters *(Yasuho Izawa)*

The 25th Sentai won another major victory against the Fourteenth Air Force over Hankow on 6 May 1944. That day, leading ace Lt Moritsugu Kanai (front row, right) shot down two P-38s, and his claims are substantiated by USAAF loss records. He tallied a total of 26 victories, and survived the war. Two further aces are pictured in the back row of this photo, namely Sgt Maj Tadashi Shono (14 kills) on the far right and WO Eiji Seino (15 kills), fourth from right *(Yasuho Izawa)*

some distance from their target, the USAAF aircraft were intercepted over Dongting Hu Lake by 24 Ki-43s of the 25th Sentai, led by Maj Sakagawa – P-38 pilots of the 449th FS reported engaging around 40 'Oscars' with 30 minutes still left to run to the target area. The USAAF fighter escorts claimed the destruction of two Ki-43s, with one probable and another damaged. The 25th Sentai, however, claimed to have shot down three P-38s. Two of these victories were awarded to ace Lt Moritsugu Kanai.

Ten minutes before the raiding force reached its target, ten Ki-43s challenged five P-51Bs of the 76th FS in a head-on pass. The US fighters were led by legendary ace Col 'Tex' Hill. One Mustang was shot down in the dogfight that ensued, with a second one damaged. Maj Sakagawa claimed three kills and a second 25th Sentai pilot was credited with two more. It was during this battle that Hill scored the last of his 14.75 victories. One Ki-43 was lost and three damaged.

Ichi-Go commenced on 26 May when 60,000 troops of the Eleventh Army marched out of Hankow and headed for the Chinese-held city of Changsha. The following day, the 25th Sentai claimed three P-40Ns destroyed whilst protecting river traffic from being strafed.

With the fighting on the ground intensifying in June, both Ki-43 sentais found themselves in regular contact with USAAF and CAF aircraft. Although giving a good account of themselves, five 'Oscar' pilots perished during the course of the month. The high point in terms of victories came on 11 June when the 48th Sentai claimed three kills.

As the battle for Hengyang intensified during mid June, both Ki-43 sentais moved closer to the fighting with a transfer to Bailuoji. From here, they would fly several ground support missions per day. Regularly tangling with USAAF fighters, 25th Sentai pilots engaged eight P-51s that were escorting four B-25s over Hengyang on the morning of 5 July. They claimed to have downed two P-51s, but Cpl Shoji Kanayama was killed. The opposing fighters were actually P-40s from the 75th FS, whose pilots reported fighting with Ki-43s north of Hengyang – they claimed three kills. That afternoon, 17 Ki-43s of the 25th Sentai fought a 20-minute battle with US fighters and claimed two P-40s destroyed.

On 11 July the 48th Sentai made five claims, followed by seven more

on 8 August – the day Japanese forces finally captured Hengyang. It had three pilots killed and sentai CO Maj Masao Matsuo badly wounded on this date, however. Nine Ki-43s were also destroyed at the unit's Bailuoji base, forcing its withdrawal from combat to recuperate. The 48th had claimed 35 kills in three months of fighting, but at a cost of 16 pilots.

Maj Toshio Sakagawa taxies out in his Ki-43-II at Hankow on 13 July 1944, shortly before the ace was posted to Akeno, in Japan, to become deputy commander of the 200th Sentai *(Yasuho Izawa)*

25th Sentai CO Maj Toshio Sakagawa was also removed from the China front at this time, having claimed 15 kills. Recalled to the Akeno Fighter School, he was eventually made deputy commander of the specially enlarged 200th Sentai, which fought in the Philippines. Sakagawa was killed here on 19 December 1944 when the transport aircraft in which he was flying crashed during a night take-off from Negros.

The 25th Sentai had prospered under Sakagawa's leadership, with a comparison of JAAF victory claims with Allied loss records showing that between 23 July 1942 and 25 July 1944, the unit shot down a total of 44 aircraft – 18 P-40s, 11 P-38s, six B-24s, four P-66s, three P-51s and two P-43s. A further 39 aircraft (25 P-40s, five B-24s, five P-38s, two P-51s, one P-43 and one P-66) were downed in air combats in which the sentai participated with other JAAF units. It can therefore be estimated that the actual total of aerial victories attributable to the 25th Sentai was 50 to 70.

In return, it lost 48 pilots over the same period. Of this number, 23 were killed in combat with P-40s, eight to P-40s or P-51s, three to P-51s, two to P-38s and one to a P-38 or a P-51. One Ki-43 pilot fell victim to defensive fire from a B-25, another to a B-24 and a third to flak. Two died on the ground in bombing attacks and six were killed in flying accidents.

The *Ichi-Go* offensive continued after the fall of Hengyang, and the 25th Sentai continued to see sporadic action against USAAF fighters and, very occasionally, B-29s that were now flying from bases in China. The unit continued to suffer losses too, as the P-51B in particular began to prevail over the increasingly obsolescent Ki-43-II. Amongst those pilots

This group of 25th Sentai/1st Chutai pilots includes three aces. They are, front row (from left to right), WO Iwataro Hazawa (15 victories), Capt Hiroshi Kusano (1st Chutai leader from September 1944 to war's end), WO Tadao Tashiro (eight victories) and Sgt Maj Kyushiro Ohtake (15 victories). The two men standing in the back row are unidentified *(Yasuho Izawa)*

killed were two sentai commanders, a chutai leader and eight-victory ace, and hikotei leader, Capt Takashi Tsuchiya, who fell in combat over Yuezhou on 3 September.

In an effort to restore parity with Allied fighters in China, the sentai re-equipped with the new Ki-43-III and a handful of Ki-84s in early November. The 48th Sentai also returned to Wuchang at this time, and claimed a number of P-51s destroyed during a strafing mission to Hengyang on 9 November. It lost four fighters and a pilot the following day, however, when a formation

was bounced by Mustangs, and a further six Ki-43s were destroyed on the ground at Wuchang during a strafing attack.

Further losses were suffered on 18 December during yet more USAAF attacks on Wuchang and Hankow, with the 25th Sentai having a pilot killed and its CO, Maj Katsuimi

The Ki-43-II of 25th Sentai/2nd Chutai ace Sgt Maj Kyushiro Ohtake taxies at Nanking in early 1945. Having served operationally in China from March 1941, Ohtake was seriously wounded on 13 August 1945 in combat over Seoul. Forced to bale out of his blazing Hayabusa, he eventually succumbed to his injuries in 1951 *(Yasuho Izawa)*

Mukaidani, and aces WOs Tadao Tashiro and Eiji Seino wounded. The latter had intercepted B-29s and their P-51 escorts over Hankow, claiming a Mustang shot down prior to being wounded in the left leg after being set upon by three more fighters. Seino crash-landed and returned to his unit after a month in hospital. Having lost most of its 'Oscars' in this raid, the 25th sent the majority of its pilots back to Japan to collect new Ki-43-IIIs.

Only a handful of personnel remained at Hengyang, and at dawn on 4 January 1945, three of them – aces Sgt Maj Kyushiro Ohtake and the now recovered WO Tashiro, and Lt Masao Hideshima – were sent on a suicidal attack on Laohekou airfield. Ohtake aborted due to a technical problem with his 'Oscar', but Tashiro and Hideshima attacked the target with Ta Dan bombs. Both men were then shot down and killed by P-51s.

Ten days later, the 48th lost three pilots and six aircraft and the 25th two pilots whilst intercepting USAAF fighters and bombers sent to attack Hankow and Wuchang. Amongst the latter was 15-kill ace Lt Iwataro Hazawa, whose aircraft was hit as he was climbing to intercept the enemy formation. With his Ki-43 on fire, Hazawa baled out over Hankow, but the ripcord of his parachute had been severed and he fell to his death.

These clashes on 14 January were the last large-scale actions involving Ki-43s in China, and later that month the 25th moved to Nanking when the 5th Air Army was ordered to prepare for the expected US invasion of China's east coast. The 48th remained assigned to the 13th Air Division in Hankow, however, transferring to Nanking in May and operating from here until war's end. The 25th eventually moved from Nanking to Suwon, in Korea, in June in preparation for the invasion of Japan. One of the unit's final combats took place over the Korean city of Taegu on 24 July when ace Lt Moritsugu Kanai intercepted B-24s and claimed several damaged. The unit also suffered its last combat fatality during this mission. The 25th remained in Korea until the cessation of hostilities.

The only other 'Oscar' unit to see action in this theatre in the final months of the war was the 24th Sentai, which moved to Hong Kong from Formosa on 7 February 1945. Using Swatow as its base, the sentai claimed three B-24s and a P-51 destroyed for the loss of two pilots prior to returning to Formosa on 25 March.

25th Sentai/3rd Chutai leader Capt Keisaku Motohashi leads two more Hayabusas out at the start of a mission from Hankow in mid 1944. The middle Ki-43-II was piloted by Cpl Haruyuki Todai, while ace 2Lt Iwataro Hazawa was at the controls of '51'. Both Motohashi and Hazawa would later perish in combat *(Yasuho Izawa)*

GREEN HELL OF NEW GUINEA

When, on 22 and 23 December 1942, Ki-43 pilots of the JAAF's 11th Sentai failed to down a B-17 from the 43rd BG that was flying reconnaissance missions over the IJN base of Rabaul, in New Britain, they were ridiculed by their Navy counterparts. The heavy bomber seemed to be totally immune to the 12.7 mm guns fitted to 'Oscars', even though they fired all of their ammunition at it.

Yet it was the IJN that had requested the JAAF's support in the South West Pacific area at a time when its units were engaged in heavy fighting with US forces for possession of the Solomon Islands, and in particular Guadalcanal. Land-based naval aviation units had suffered serious losses in the Solomons and New Guinea, and therefore needed the help of JAAF squadrons pulled from Burma and Indochina.

The first JAAF unit – the 12th Hiko-dan, comprising its headquarters and the 1st and 11th Sentais – arrived in-theatre on 18 December. The latter unit had collected 60 Ki-43-Is from the 50th and 64th Sentais prior to boarding a small aircraft carrier and sailing for Truk Atoll, in the western Pacific. From here, the 11th Sentai would be led by IJN G4M 'Betty' bombers to Vunakanau airfield, on Rabaul, on the 18th.

Many of the sentai's pilots were old hands, and some, including aces Lt Tomoari Hasegawa and WOs Naoharu Shiromoto, Haruo Takagaki and Tokuyasu Ishizuka, had participated in the Nomonhan Incident. As an advance unit, the 11th was at double its normal strength.

The 1st Chutai, led by Capt Shigenori Miyabayashi, was the first JAAF unit to become active in New Guinea. Its 15 Ki-43s made a strafing attack on Buna South airfield (Dobodura) on 26 December, where pilots found RAAF Hudsons on the runway and immediately attacked them. They were in turn surprised by four P-40Es of the 9th FS/49th FG, which had been recalled by Dobodura control. The Warhawk pilots claimed to have downed five Ki-43s, although only Sgt Majs Fujii and Imamura failed to return. The sentai in turn claimed six P-40s destroyed, although only one was shot down – the aircraft flown by ace Lt John Landers.

The 1st Chutai returned to Buna two days later, this time accompanied by IJN Zero-sens, and its pilots claimed seven P-38s destroyed for a

Brand new Ki-43-Is of the 1st Sentai formate for the camera during the unit's transition training period at Akeno in mid 1942. The bars painted on the rudder – white outlined in yellow – denote the 2nd flight of the 1st Sentai's 1st Chutai. These aircraft would be sent to New Guinea in January 1943 (*Yasuho Izawa*)

73

11th Sentai/1st Chutai ace
Lt Hironojo Shishimoto engaged a
P-38 over Lae on 31 December 1942
and claimed to have shot it down,
although his own aircraft was so
badly damaged in the process that
he had to take to his parachute.
The Lightning was the first of 11
kills and seven probables credited
to Shishimoto, who also also fought
with the 11th over China and the
Philippines (*Yasuho Izawa*)

single loss. On 31 December, whilst flying as Capt Miyabayashi's wing-man, Nomonhan ace Lt Hasegawa had his fighter shot up by a P-38 in combat off Lae, and he forced landed at Gasmata. He returned to base several days later. Future 11-kill ace Lt Hironojo Shishimoto scored his first victory during this engagement when he claimed a P-38 destroyed.

On 5 January 1943, a patrol from the now operational 2nd Chutai intercepted B-17s attacking its Rabaul base at 0728 hrs and claimed one probable. At 1020 hrs six more B-17s from the 43rd BG, accompanied by six B-24s of the 90th BG, attacked a large convoy of cargo ships and destroyers in Rabaul harbour that were getting ready to head to Lae and Salamaua, in northern New Guinea.

The Ki-43 pilots had learned from their earlier humiliating failures against the 'heavies', and had trained in the meantime to perfect head-on attacks that targeted bomber pilots and the engines of their aircraft. Fighters of the 2nd Chutai were scrambled. Meanwhile, those that had been assigned to provide top cover for the convoy became aware that their charges were under attack when they saw bomb splashes near the vessels. WO Kaminoto claimed one B-17, but 15-kill Nomonhan ace Sgt Maj Haruo Takagaki was shot down in flames. Taking to his parachute, he was plucked out of the water and returned to base. Finally, 2Lt Kotobuki Nagayo chased a bomber too far on his own and was killed. The 11th Sentai claimed two B-17s destroyed and two B-24s as probables.

Actual 43rd BG losses were two B-17Fs, with Capt Jack Albert ditching near the Trobriand Islands, allowing his crew to be rescued. The second bomber, piloted by Maj Allan Lindbergh, crashed in flames, taking V Bomber Command CO Brig Gen Kenneth Walker with it.

In this engagement the 11th Sentai's pilots had been able to demonstrate to their IJN counterparts the real hitting power of their 12.7 mm guns, as well as their skill in combat with US heavy bombers.

Having defended the convoy in Rabual, the 11th duly escorted the vessels to Lae between 5 and 10 January. The ships were carrying a large expeditionary force that was needed to relieve the garrisons in northern New Guinea, and the Allies threw everything they had at them. The sentai flew 283 sorties during this five-day period, claiming 15 victories, but at a cost of 23 Ki-43s destroyed and six pilots killed.

Although badly mauled, the JAAF's fighter force received a boost on 9 January when 33 Ki-43s of the 1st Sentai arrived from Indochina to reinforce Rabaul's air defences. Its arrival allowed the 11th Sentai to move forward to Buka Island. The 1st followed suit when it transferred to Ballale. These moves were made so that the JAAF could help cover the Japanese Army's withdrawal from Guadalcanal, planned for 1 February.

The first missions flown by the fighter sentais over the beleaguered island occurred on 27 January, when the 1st and 11th sent 30 Ki-43s to cover nine Ki-48s from the 45th Sentai that were attempting to bomb advancing US troops. Six P-38s of the 339th FS engaged the JAAF formation, followed by eight US Navy F4Fs. Ten P-40s also joined in, and two were shot down. The rear guard 11th Sentai's 3rd Chutai then engaged the P-38s and the Wildcats in a 15-minute running dogfight. Two Lightnings were shot down and an F4F ran out of fuel and ditched.

The US defenders claimed ten 'Zeros' for the loss of two P-40s (plus two more in landing mishaps), two P-38s and an F4F. The 1st and 11th Sentais in turn claimed two P-38s, three P-39s and one F4F destroyed for the loss of a Ki-43 shot down, another crash-landing and four posted as missing. Four 1st Sentai pilots were killed, including Sgt Haruo Sato, who had shot down a PBY Catalina on 7 December 1941 just prior to the attack on Pearl Harbor. He had therefore become the first Japanese fighter pilot to destroy an Allied aircraft in World War 2.

A 1st Sentai/3rd Chutai Ki-43-I is seen flying a patrol from Rabaul in early January 1943. The unit was sent into action over Guadalacanal later that same month (*Yasuho Izawa*)

The heavy losses sustained over Guadalcanal by the 1st Sentai had shaken the pilots' confidence, as they had previously considered themselves to be the best in the JAAF.

On the 31st, the 11th Sentai's 3rd Chutai engaged eight F4Fs that were escorting 12 SBDs sent to attack Japanese troopships in the Gizo Strait, some 250 miles west of Guadalcanal. Two F4Fs were shot down by future 13-kill ace WO Takeo Takahashi, although four Ki-43 pilots were killed in return. That same day, the 1st Sentai attempted to scramble three fighters from Ballale to intercept incoming P-38s, but only ace WO Naoharu Shiromoto succeeded in getting airborne. Flying headlong into a formation of 20+ fighters, he shot down two P-38s and caused two more to collide, before managing to land back at base – his victories were confirmed by Japanese troops in the Munda area.

The next day the IJN started its first withdrawal of troops from Guadalcanal. That morning, 23 Ki-43s of the 11th Sentai escorted six 45th Sentai Ki-48s sent to attack Guadalcanal's second airfield in an effort to keep US aircraft away from the evacuation vessels. The sentai claimed four P-40 victories after encountering the 44th FS near Savo Island.

The second evacuation took place on 4 February, and JAAF fighter pilots assumed responsibility for escorting the fleet from IJN A6M units, which had suffered heavy losses three days earlier. For this mission, the 11th Sentai re-located from Rabaul to Munda airfield. The unit fought a series of running battle with US Navy, Marine Corps and USAAF aircraft during the course of the day as it attempted to protect 21 IJN destroyer-transporters that had departed Shortland Island at 0930 hrs. During early afternoon skirmishes, the Ki-43 pilots claimed one P-40, two F4Fs and a pair of SBDs destroyed. In return, Sgt Koji Aoyama was lost.

Five aircraft from the 1st Chutai, supported by 1st Sentai aircraft, intercepted F4Fs, SBDs and P-39s later that afternoon. The units claimed to have downed two SBDs and an F4F for the loss of 11th Sentai pilot Cpl Tomohiro. The air battles had raged from 1352 hrs to 1545 hrs, but the combined efforts of the JAAF and IJN fighter pilots had allowed 10,650 soldiers to be safely evacuated.

On 6 February, the 11th Sentai turned its attention to New Guinea, when 29 Ki-43s escorted nine 45th Sentai Ki-48s to Wau. Few worth-while ground targets were found, however. Pilots of the 3rd Chutai had to be content with shooting down a C-47 from the 33rd TCS, as well as an RAAF Boston. While providing top cover, the Ki-43s of the 1st and 2nd Chutais were jumped by P-38s and P-40s, and four Ki-43s were shot

1st Sentai commander Maj Mitsugu Sawada reported shooting down a B-17 while escorting a convoy on 1 March 1943, but he was killed four days later while single-handedly fighting P-38s and P-40s in a Ki-43 with a non-retractable undercarriage. One of the JAAF's leading fighter pilots pre-war, Sawada had claimed seven victories in China between 1937 and 1941 (*Yasuho Izawa*)

down. Amongst those killed was sentai CO, Maj Katsuji Sugiura – three Ki-48s were also destroyed to complete a major victory for the USAAF. In return, 17-kill Nomonhan ace WO Haruo Takagaki claimed two Lightnings for his only confirmed successes in World War 2. The 11th Sentai claimed ten P-38s destroyed in total following this mission.

Just under a month later, on 5 March, during yet another escort mission for a convoy heading to Lae, the JAAF lost newly arrived 1st Sentai CO, and 11-victory Nomonhan ace, Maj Mitsugu Sawada. Having taken off on his own from Lae, bound for Rabaul, he found that the undercarriage of his Ki-43 would not retract. Instead of returning to base, Sawada pressed on for home, and was intercepted by P-38s and P-40s. He is believed to have accounted for three of his attackers before being shot down, these kills being added to a B-17 that he had destroyed over Lae on 1 March. Sawada had only been in New Guinea for five days.

With Guadalcanal evacuated, the JAAF now turned its attention to New Guinea. In order to provide better protection for vulnerable IJN convoys re-supplying Japanese troops via north coast ports, and to act as escorts for bombers striking at Allied bases on the island, the 11th Sentai was moved to Wewak, on New Guinea's north coast, in March.

Following little aerial action in-theatre during March and April 1943, early May saw the 'Oscar' force in New Guinea strengthened with the arrival of the 24th Sentai's 1st Chutai from Sumatra – the rest of the unit flew to newly opened But East later in the month. Recently equipped with Ki-43-IIs, the chutai went into action from Babo, on the western tip of New Guinea, on the 4th, when future 16-kill ace WO Mitsuo Ogura claimed two B-24s destroyed and a third one damaged. He had scrambled when Babo was attacked, and it took him an hour to catch the bombers.

Another USAAF 'heavy' was claimed four days later by the 11th Sentai, although this time its pilot did not live to tell the tale. Whilst providing cover for two small cargo vessels bound for Madang, three Ki-43s of the 1st Chutai's third element became separated from the rest of the force and spotted a B-17 600 ft below them. The fighter pilots made repeated head-on passes at the 63rd BS bomber, which attempted to escape at low altitude, trailing black smoke from two engines.

Sgt Tadao Oda eventually rammed the bomber to prevent its crew reporting the location of the two ships carrying vital earth-moving equipment, together with 500 personnel of the 11th Airfield Construction Unit. Oda, who was the first JAAF pilot to undertake a ramming attack, was posthumously promoted two ranks. He was also the 11th Sentai's last casualty prior to the unit returning to Japan on 19 June.

The 11th Sentai had lost 19 pilots and claimed 28 Allied aircraft destroyed in New Guinea between 26 December 1942 and 8 May 1943. But East only ten of these claims – four B-17s, two P-40s, two P-38s and a Hudson and C-47 – were confirmed by Allied loss reports. In addition, two F4Fs, two SBDs, one P-40 and one TBF were shot down in the two air battles in which the 11th Sentai participated with other units.

JAAF fighter units were locked in a desperate battle with Allied air forces in the New Guinea area, and they would eventually suffer losses several times those sustained in the China-Burma-India (CBI) theatre. Their victory claims would also be over-inflated by a similar margin. JAAF fighter pilots would claim many victories at times when actual

Allied losses were nil. As it happens, USAAF fighter pilots in New Guinea and the South West Pacific area also tended to over-claim to a greater extent than their counterparts in the CBI.

By the time the 11th Sentai left New Guinea, the 24th Sentai had already seen more than a month of combat. On 23 May, another of its Nomonhan aces in the form of WO Katsuaki Kira also claimed a B-24 destroyed after attacking a trio of bombers that he had intercepted off Madang no fewer than eight times in an hour-long engagement. Three days later, Sgt Maj Naoji Menya claimed to have downed four Liberators during the seven attacking passes he made on a formation of 'heavies' he too had found off Madang.

WO Ogura claimed two more kills on 12 June when he downed a pair of P-38s north of Kainants with just 32 rounds. Wounded during this brief action, Ogura was duly hospitalised for a month.

Eight days later, the Timor-based 59th Sentai participated in the first JAAF strike on Darwin, Australia. The pioneer 'Oscar' unit had seen action over the East Indies since converting to the Ki-43-II four months earlier. Amongst those to claim victories with the 59th in early 1943 was future 14-kill ace Sgt Maj Tomio Hirohata, who downed two Lockheed bombers for his first victories. Ace Lt Hiroshi Onozaki also enjoyed success, sharing two B-25s with his wingman.

Onozaki was an element leader during the 20 June raid on Darwin, with fellow aces Capt Shigeo Nango and WO Kazuo Shimizu also taking part in this mission. Some 22 Ki-43s rendezvoused with 18 Ki-49s of the 61st Sentai over Timor at 0730 hrs. Nine Ki-48s from the 75th Sentai would also be involved in the attack. 1st Chutai leader Lt Shigeki Nanba spotted hostile activity to the south soon after passing Bathurst Island, and the covering force from the 2nd and 3rd Chutais engaged the interceptors. Three bombers would be lost to the defending RAF and

A Ki-43-II from the 24th Sentai takes off from But East airstrip, near Wewak, in May 1943 (*Yasuho Izawa*)

These Ki-43-IIs of the 24th Sentai were also photographed at But East. Note the sentai insignia in chutai colours on their tails (*Yasuho Izawa*)

59th Sentai 14-kill ace Sgt Maj Tomio Hirohata (far left) and his groundcrew pose with their uniquelly marked Ki-43-II at But, in New Guinea, in October 1943. Hirohata saw considerable action in this theatre with the 59th between March 1943 and February 1944, when the unit returned to Japan. He would subsequently perish attempting to bale out of a Ki-61 that had suffered mechanical problems on 22 April 1945. By then Hirohata had seen five continuous years of service with the 59th Sentai (*Hirohata family via Yasuho Izawa*)

The 59th Sentai's leading ace of the early months of World War 2 (he had claimed 11 kills by mid March 1942), Lt Hiroshi Onozaki claimed three more victories with the unit in New Guinea prior to being struck down by amoebic dysentery in late August 1943. He was duly evacuated home, and after recovering, Onozaki served as an instructor for the rest of the war (*Yasuho Izawa*)

RAAF Spitfires, and the Ki-43 pilots would claim nine Allied fighters shot down in return – only two were actually destroyed. Amongst the pilots claiming kills was Lt Onozaki, who was credited with two Spitfires shot down. Capt Nango led a fighter sweep near Darwin two days later, but no Allied aircraft were encountered.

In mid July the 59th Sentai was ordered to move from Lautuen, in Timor, to But East. The unit replaced the 11th Sentai, which had departed in late June, and the 1st Sentai, which left during August.

The JAAF had more than just the Allies to contend with in New Guinea, as 60 per cent of its aircrew at Wewak reported sick during the summer of 1943. Most were suffering from malaria or amoebic dysentery, including Lt Onozaki, who was struck down by the latter shortly after he had claimed a P-38 over Tsili Tsili for his 14th victory on 15 August. Another pilot to enjoy success on this date was 59th Sentai, 2nd Chutai leader Capt Nango. Both he and Onozaki were part of a formation of 22 Ki-43s from the unit, together with 14 'Oscars' from the 24th, that rendezvoused with seven Ki-48s of the 208th Sentai over Wewak prior to heading to Allied airfields in Fubua. At 0830 hrs, the fighter pilots sighted 30 Allied machines climbing towards the bombers. Capt Shigeki Nanba was flying as part of the top cover, and he recalled;

'The escort fighters were far behind at that time. Then the six Ki-43s of my 1st Chutai quickly dived to attack, but it was too late, as one by one the Ki-48s were shot down in flames. Our fighters drove off the P-40s and P-39s that climbed away, rather than attempting to escape down the narrow valley. When they disappeared, we found some "DC-3s" attempting to land. We jumped them and claimed three or four.'

Four P-39s were also shot down, as was a single C-47 of the 374th TCG. Another transport vanished into the surrounding mountains and was never found. Capt Nango claimed one P-40 and a transport. He had attacked the latter from such close range that oil from his victim was smeared all over his Ki-43. Assuming that the fluid was leaking from his own engine, and that it was therefore on the verge of seizing, Nango was on the point of placing his aircraft into a final suicide dive when he realised that he still had full control of his machine. Nanba remembered;

'As I watched, my wingman, Sgt Umeya, warned me by radio that a P-40 was about to jump me. I was able to avoid it and send a burst into the diving P-40. When I was ordered to return, I saw a Ki-43 tenaciously chasing a P-40 at low altitude, and I provided cover for him. It was Capt Nango. We later returned home together, his fighter covered in oil.'

A follow-up mission to Fubua was flown on 16 August, and over the next two days the 24th and 59th Sentais claimed 39 kills. This was to be the last large-scale success enjoyed by the JAAF in New Guinea.

During the night of 16/17 August, 50+ B-17s and B-24s attacked Wewak airfield, and its satellites at Boram and But East. The USAAF bombers struck a telling blow, as most of the Ki-43s assigned to the 59th Sentai's 3rd Chutai were destroyed on the ground. The bombers had not finished, however, for a group of B-25s then attacked the bases at low-level and inflicted yet more damage. As a result of these raids, the JAAF's 4th Air Force lost some 50 aircraft, with another 50 damaged. These attacks signalled the start of a campaign to neutralise Japanese airfields in preparation for an offensive on Lae.

That same day the 1st Sentai returned to Japan, leaving all of its Ki-43s at Rabaul. The unit had lost six pilots in air combat between 27 January and 16 August 1943. Having seen all of its Ki-45s destroyed in the Wewak attacks, the 13th Sentai began operating the 'Oscars' left behind by the 1st.

The JAAF suffered a further blow in 20 August when 28-victory WO Chiyoji Saito of the 24th Sentai was killed in combat. Having claimed 21 victories in the Nomonhan Incident, he had then seen action with the unit in the Philippines, China and, finally, New Guinea. On 10 July 1943 Saito collided with 1st Chutai CO Lt Tadashi Koga whilst landing at But East in clouds of dust. Saito was badly injured and Koga killed, and the ace told fellow pilots that he felt responsible for the accident. Saito stated that he would not return to Japan alive, and after being discharged from hospital he fought with such recklessness that he was dubbed the 'P-38 killer'. Intercepting B-24s and P-38s over Wewak on 20 August, Saito crashed to his death in the sea after being attacked by a Lightning.

All three sentais in New Guinea suffered terrible losses during August, with 20 pilots being killed in combat. In return, the units claimed 19 victories on 18 August (only one P-38 was actually lost) and 15 on the 21st (four P-38s actually destroyed).

At dawn on 2 September, five IJN cargo vessels loaded with vital supplies for JAAF units in New Guinea arrived off Wewak. When a patrolling Ki-46 radioed at 0740 hrs that a large enemy formation was heading north, all 36 operational fighters of the 14th Hiko-dan (the fighter sentais' controlling unit) were ordered to take off. Around 30 P-38s arrived at 0900 hrs, and while they were being engaged by JAAF fighters, 30+ B-25s roared in from the east and southeast at low altitude, heading for the ships. One vessel was sunk and two damaged before the attack had ended.

Ki-43-IIs of the 24th Sentai sit idle at But East. This airstrip on the northern New Guinea coastline was carved out of the jungle by Japanese Army engineers in early 1943, and the 24th was the first unit to take up residence in May of that year. Note that all the 'Oscars' are equipped with two drop tanks apiece (*Yasuho Izawa*)

Seen here in China during the Nomonhan Incident, these 24th Sentai aces are, from left to right, WOs Katsuaki Kira (standing, who claimed 21 enemy aircraft in total, and survived the war), Chiyoji Saito (sitting in vehicle, who scored 28 aerial victories and was killed over Wewak on 20 August 1943) and Koji Ishizawa (sitting, centre). The latter claimed at least 11 kills in 1939, and survived the war (*Yasuho Izawa*)

The P-38 pilots also claimed to have shot down ten JAAF interceptors. Three Ki-43 pilots were killed and two Ki-61s and a Ki-43 crash-landed. Three more fighters were damaged. The surviving Japanese fighter pilots filed claims for five P-38s and six B-25s destroyed – three B-25Ds had in fact been shot down. Just as serious as losing six valuable aircraft and three pilots was the loss to the JAAF of a significant quantity of fuel and valuable aircraft drop tanks held as cargo in the sunken and damaged ships.

The following day Allied forces landed at Hopoi, east of Lae, and on the 22nd more troops came ashore at Finschhafen, northeast of Hopoi. The fighter sentais put what meagre forces they had into the air in an effort to repel the landings, but they suffered still more losses.

To make matters worse, by late September most JAAF aircrew in New Guinea had succumbed to malaria or amoebic dysentery, but only those sufferers who were actually feverish were excused from flying combat missions. The morale of the fighter units was sapped as their strength fell.

At month end the 59th Sentai was ordered to Manila for recuperation, and its 15 remaining Ki-43s were handed over to the 14th Hikodan. The 24th Sentai also left, returning to Japan on 2 October after passing its 11 Ki-43s on to the 13th and 68th Sentais. The 24th had claimed 80 aerial victories in New Guinea since May, but had lost 20 pilots in the process.

On the morning of 11 October, a formation of Ki-43s led by 14th Hikodan CO Lt Col Tamiya Teranishi was jumped by four P-47s from the 348th FG while flying at 19,500 ft. JAAF groundcrew who had been watching the air battle heard the rumbling of 0.50-in machine guns and the sound of unfamiliar engines. They had been listening to the first engagement between Ki-43s and the Thunderbolt. It ended with two 'Oscars' plunging in flames into Wewak Bay. Future Pacific theatre P-47 ace Col Neel Kearby was credited with shooting down four Ki-43s. Lt Col Teranishi and Capt Koyama were killed, and the aircraft of wingman Sgt Haraguchi was damaged and forced to crash-land on the airfield.

Better success came the Ki-43's way on 16 October, when 13th Sentai pilots, flying alongside Ki-61s of the 68th Sentai, claimed five B-25s destroyed when the latter attacked Boram and Wewak airfields. The JAAF lost two Ki-43s and one Ki-61, and their pilots, in return.

On the 20th, the JAAF's 4th Air Force began to comply with an 18th Army request to drop food supplies for troops of the 20th Division fighting Allied ground forces in the Finschhafen area. The 18th had asked for three tons to be dropped each day for ten days, and two bombers

These 24th Sentai pilots survived five months' of combat over New Guinea between May and October 1943. They claimed 80 aerial victories during this period for the loss of 20 pilots. This photograph was taken at Ashiya airfield, in Japan in December 1943. The individual in full uniform in the centre of the photograph is sentai CO, Maj Shoichi Tashiro, who led the unit from August 1943 through to December 1944 (*Yasuho Izawa*)

attempted to fly dawn sorties between the 23rd and the 25th. One was lost on the 24th, so the 4th Air Force decided to deploy nine Ki-49 heavy bombers, escorted by 25 fighters, to make daytime drops on the 27th. Intercepted by P-39s, three Ki-49s and two 13th Sentai Ki-43s were lost. The JAAF claimed to have downed 13 US aircraft, but only one Airacobra was destroyed. These losses convinced the 4th Air Force that a viable air supply operation was impossible in the face of Allied air superiority.

The 59th Sentai returned to New Guinea on 31 October with 23 Ki-43-IIs. On the way it lost its veteran CO, Maj Takeo Fukuda, who crashed due to engine failure, so leadership of the unit fell to deputy CO Capt Shigeo Nango, whose exploits in the theatre had become legendary. Fellow ace Capt Yasuhiko Kuroe wrote of him, 'He was smart and tall. He was cheerful, unselfish, intrepid, and he didn't put on any airs, so he was loved by superiors and subordinates alike to an uncommon degree.'

On 6 November, 22 of the unit's fighters joined 30 newly-arrived Ki-43s of the 248th Sentai (formerly defending the home islands), together with 15 more from the 13th and nine Ki-61s of the 78th Sentai, in meeting ten Ki-21s of the 14th Sentai over Wewak. Their objective was Nadzab airfield, which they bombed. They also engaged Allied fighters, claiming several shot down for the loss of a 248th Sentai machine.

Three days later, 55 JAAF fighters left Wewak, and over Madang 20 Ki-43s of the 59th Sentai engaged 80 Allied bombers and fighters, while another force of 35 fighters clashed with 40 enemy machines – three were actually lost. Some 25 Allied aircraft were claimed to have been destroyed, but the 59th lost four Ki-43s and the 248th three. Two more crash-landed. Amongst those claiming kills was ace WO Kazuo Shimizu, who attacked six P-40s single-handedly and was credited with downing one.

Between 22-26 November, the JAAF's 6th Air Division supported the 18th Army's operations in the Finschhafen area. Ki-48s and Ki-49s were escorted during a series of missions, and a handful of Allied aircraft claimed as victories for the loss of six Ki-43s. At month-end the 13th Sentai was withdrawn from eastern New Guinea and sent west to Wakde. It had operated a mixed force of Ki-45s and Ki-43s during its previous six months in combat, and had lost 18 pilots killed. By the time it was withdrawn, the 13th's operational strength had been reduced to 16 pilots.

Three B-24s were shot down over Wewak on 1 December when 20 Ki-43s and 14 Ki-61s intercepted 40 bombers and their P-47 escorts. The latter claimed to have downed 11 JAAF fighters, while their Japanese opponents reported destroying three B-24s and two P-47s. The 248th Sentai lost a Ki-43, and 11 more aircraft were destroyed on the ground.

On 15 December yet another Allied landing occurred, this time at Arawe, on the southwestern tip of New Britain. JAAF bombers were immediately despatched, with Capt Nango of the 59th Sentai leading the fighter escorts. His aircraft were overwhelmed by Lightnings patrolling the beachhead, and Nango confided to his diary that evening, 'We are being made fools of by the P-38s. It is difficult to keep on fighting them with the Ki-43s'. As if to emphasise this point, on the 16th five bombers and five Ki-43 and Ki-61 escorts were downed by P-38s.

The 68th Sentai lost its ranking ace, Capt Shogo Takeuchi, on 21 December whilst escorting bombers sent to attack troops at Arawe. With his unit reduced to just three fit pilots, Takeuchi, who was flying a Ki-61,

59th Sentai ace and 2nd Chutai leader Capt Shigeo Nango joined the unit in January 1942, but did not see any real action until the JAAF attacks on Port Darwin in June of the following year. He was a younger brother of the legendary IJN fighter pilot Lt Cdr Mochifumi Nango, who had shot down eight Chinese aircraft by the time he was killed in a mid-air collision with another enemy machine over Nanking on 18 July 1938. One of the most respected, and capable, JAAF fighter pilots to see combat in New Guinea, Nango's tally stood at 15 victories when he was killed in combat over Wewak on 23 January 1944 *(Yasuho Izawa)*

was seen to down an F4F for his 19th kill and then head for Hansa airfield. Just before landing his engine cut and his aircraft overturned and hit trees. Takeuchi died three hours later. Although flying the Ki-61 in New Guinea, Takeuchi had claimed many kills in the Ki-43 with the 64th Sentai over Malaya, Singapore and the East Indies prior to joining the 68th.

More Allied landings occurred in late December and early January, and although the JAAF did its best to oppose these, the growing strength of enemy air power resulted in yet more defeats. The 248th Sentai lost its CO, Maj Shin-ichi Muraoka, on 2 January whilst attacking the new beachhead at Saidor. The unit had claimed 97 aircraft destroyed or damaged for the loss of 17 Ki-43s by then. The following day, the 63rd Sentai arrived at Wewak from Japan, bringing with it 27 Ki-43-IIs.

All four available fighter sentais attacked Nadzab on 15 January, Capt Shigeo Nango encountering four P-40s over the target area and claiming three of them shot down. The lead P-40 was destroyed by Nango's wingman. All told, JAAF fighter pilots claimed eight kills, but the author has been unable to find any confirmatory Allied loss reports. The next day, the 63rd Sentai became engaged in a fierce battle near Madang during which it claimed two Allied aircraft, but lost five Ki-43s in the process.

The 59th Sentai suffered a grave loss on 23 January when Capt Nango was killed whilst attacking a large Allied formation over Wewak. Some 35 B-24s and their escorts claimed 12 Japanese fighters for the loss of five of their own. The JAAF claimed 18 and lost seven fighters. Having led the sentai in almost every mission it had undertaken in-theatre, Nango was referred to by senior officers as 'He who maintains the air battle of New Guinea for the Japanese Army'. The 59th had claimed 90+ kills by the time of Nango's demise, of which he had personally scored at least 15.

Rocked by the loss of its most experienced leader, the 59th left Hollandia for Japan on 17 February. Just prior to its departure, the unit's ranking New Guinea ace, WO Kazuo Shimizu, employed the Ta Dan incendiary/fragmentation bomb to good effect when he claimed two B-25s destroyed on 14 February. The following day, he claimed two P-47s with the same weapon. These took Shimizu's tally of kills to 18.

The 59th's place was taken in Hollandia by two battle-hardened Ki-43 units in the form of the 33rd Sentai, on 22 February, and the 77th six days later. Both units were equipped with Ki-43-IIs. By early March they had joined in the fighting.

Despite the infusion of new units, the JAAF continued to suffer heavy losses as it tried to defend Wewak. There were occasional successes, however, as on 5 March when the 77th Sentai engaged three P-47s led by 21-victory ace Col Kearby. The latter was shot down and killed when he lost speed trying to catch a Ki-48 from the 75th Sentai. WO Koichi Mitoma and novice Sgt Hiroshi Aoyagi each claimed to have downed a P-47 over Wewak.

This mid-production Ki-43-II was assigned to 59th Sentai ace Capt Shigeo Nango in late 1943. Fitted with a single 200-litre drop tank beneath its left wing, the aircraft is being taxied out – possibly by Nango himself – at But East at the start of yet another mission (*Yasuho Izawa*)

Between 11 and 15 March, the unit's pilots claimed the destruction of nine Allied fighters and bombers, although it also had four pilots killed during the same period. Included in this number was 13-victory ace Capt Yoshiro Kuwabara, who had claimed 12 kills flying Ki-27s in 1941-42. Having downed a P-47 for his 13th success on 11 March, he was lost dogfighting with P-38s the very next day.

After 16 March the skies over Wewak were deemd to be unsafe for

High-scoring 59th Sentai ace WO Kazuo Shimizu (squatting centre, holding a placard that reads *Inouye Squadron*), is seen with other 3rd Chutai pilots at Ashiya in December 1943. Having 'made ace' in New Guinea, Shimizu duly saw further action flying Ki-61s and Ki-100s during homeland defence missions in the final months of the war. He would survive the conflict with 18 victories to his name, half of which were multi-engined bombers (*Yasuho Izawa*)

JAAF aircraft to operate in, and all units withdrew to Hollandia. On the last two days of the month, the 63rd and 77th Sentais lost most of their Ki-43s on the ground to Allied bombing. Those aircraft that survived were thrown into action on 11 April, when the 6th Air Division sortied its entire fighter strength (20 Ki-43s and Ki-61s) against B-25s and P-47s over Wewak. The Ki-43s were led by 33rd Sentai ace Capt Kiyoshi Namai. The newly arrived 58th FG was jumped by four Ki-61s and immediately lost a P-47. The fighter formation scattered and the Ki-61s and Ki-43s shot down two more Thunderbolts in what had become a one-sided contest – one of these was claimed by Capt Namai. It was the last triumph by JAAF fighter pilots in eastern New Guinea.

The USAAF bombed Hollandia on 12 and 16 April and destroyed the remaining JAAF fighter strength in New Guinea. On the 21st, US carrier-borne aircraft also attacked Hollandia. Only six Ki-43s rose to meet them, and one survived the ensuing battle – it was later destroyed on the ground. The Allied fleet then shelled Hollandia, preparatory to a landing on the 22nd. When the invaders attacked the airfield two days later, 7000 Japanese troops fled into the jungle. They left on foot with five days' food, but most of the 5000 JAAF personnel, including 70 fighter pilots, perished trying to escape from New Guinea. The 63rd, 68th, 77th, 78th and 248th Sentais were all disbanded following the fall of Hollandia.

Further west, the 13th Sentai swapped its Ki-45s for 26 Ki-43-IIs at Halmahera in April 1944, before moving to Noemfor Island. This force had been reduced to ten aircraft by the time the Allies landed on Biak Island, off northwestern New Guinea, on 27 May. The 24th Sentai moved to Halmahera at this time following its recuperation in Japan. Assigned to the IJN, the unit saw action over Biak until withdrawn to Wasile on 25 June – by then it had lost ten Ki-43s in combat.

Following incessant attacks on Biak and Halmahera, both the 13th and 24th Sentais evacuated to Ambon and the Celebes, in the East Indies, in July. They continued to fly patrols, and intercept Allied bombers, although the 'Oscars' were no match for the P-38s. Nevertheless, ranking 13th Sentai ace WO Misao Inoue managed to claim a handful of kills flying both the Ki-43 and Ki-45, and by the time he left the unit in October 1944, his score stood at 16 (half during the Nomonhan Incident). Ki-84s were issued to the 13th Sentai that same month, and both units were eventually pulled back to help defend the Philippines.

77th Sentai ace and 3rd Chutai leader Capt Youshiro Kuwabara, who was killed in combat with P-38s over Wewak on 12 March 1944 – just 24 hours after downing a P-47 for his first victory in New Guinea. All bar one of his kills were scored whilst flying Ki-27s over Thailand and Burma in 1941-42. Indeed, his tally stood at 12 victories by 26 February 1942 (*Yasuho Izawa*)

DESPERATION IN THE PHILIPPINES

Following the IJN's comprehensive defeat in the Battle of the Philippine Sea in June 1944, US forces turned their attention to liberating the Philippines from Japanese control. The JAAF reacted to this threat by bolstering its forces in the region. Amongst the units sent south from Japan were the Ki-43-II-equipped 30th and 31st Sentais of the 13th Hikodan, which reached Luzon from Manchuria in July and then moved to Negros in early August.

These units saw action for the first time on 12 September, when US Navy aircraft from various carrier air groups in the area attacked targets on Negros. The 31st claimed six kills for one loss, but the 30th lost several machines. The following day, four bomb-laden Ki-43s attempted to attack the carriers, and only one aircraft returned from this fruitless mission. US Navy fighters then attacked islands in the Visayan Sea, and the 'Oscar' pilots claimed up to ten victories. Twelve pilots were killed in return, however, with 20 Ki-43s shot down in total. Such losses hit both units hard, and by 22 September the 31st Sentai had been reduced in strength to just six serviceable aircraft.

US Navy aircraft also ventured north to Formosa on 12 October, with 32 Ki-43s from the 20th Sentai intercepting fighters and bombers as they approached Hsiaochang and Taipei. Six pilots were killed and ten 'Oscars' shot down.

Twenty-four hours prior to the devastating attack on Formosa, reinforcements had been despatched from Japan to the Philippines. The 26th Sentai was joined in Manila by the battle-hardened 204th Sentai, the latter unit having seen much action in Burma. Pilots of the 204th expected little trouble from their US opponents when they arrived in the Philippines, but they were in for a nasty shock. In their first combat on 15 October, they were jumped by F6F Hellcats when they attempted a scramble from their airfield at Nielson. Six perished, including seven-kill ace Lt Hiroshi Gomi. Four other Ki-43s were destroyed and ten more damaged on the ground. The 26th also lost three pilots, but it at least claimed four aircraft destroyed.

US forces now prepared for a landing on Leyte on 19 October,

One of only three pilots to achieve ace status with the 204th Sentai, Lt Hiroshi Gomi, who had claimed seven victories over Burma, was killed during the unit's very first combat over the Philippines on 15 October 1944 (*Yasuho Izawa*)

which would signal the start of the land battle for control of the Philippines. The Japanese Supreme Command reacted by ordering Operation *Sho Ichi-Go* to commence at midnight on the 19th. The JAAF had sent the 26th and 204th Sentais to Fabrica airfield, on Negros, 24 hours earlier, each Ki-43 flying in with a groundcrewman in the rear fuselage.

On 22 October, 18 Ki-43-IIs of the 20th Sentai were transferred to Caloocan, near Manila, from Formosa. The unit was ordered to fly convoy patrols and provide air defence for the Philippine capital. The 24th Sentai also headed to Negros from the Celebes, and the 31st was posted to Fabrica.

Between 19 and 24 October, the Negros-based Ki-43 units flew 23 bombing sorties against ships lying off Leyte. And although no 'Oscars' were shot down, only three remained in an airworthy state on Negros by the 25th following a series of raids on the island by US aircraft.

The decisive air battle of the campaign then took place over Leyte between 24 and 26 October, and it saw the JAAF's 4th Air Force lose 80 aircraft in the air and another 64 on the ground. With the Ki-43 having now been relegated to the role of fighter-bomber by the Ki-61 and Ki-84, only two 'Oscars' (from the 204th) were shot down on the 24th, although Sgt Hayashi Nakamura claimed an enemy aircraft in return. Another of the unit's Ki-43s was shot down on the 28th.

By month-end, five Ki-43 sentais in the Philippines had just 20 serviceable aircraft between them, the 24th Sentai having lost five aircraft (one on the ground), the 26th Sentai 15 (11 on the ground) and the 204th Sentai 17 (ten on the ground). On 1 November the 30th Sentai was one of four fighter units ordered back to Japan to recuperate.

That same day, a convoy carrying the Japanese Army's 1st Infantry Division entered Ormoc Bay in an attempt to relieve the situation following the US landings at Leyte. The 204th Sentai was ordered to provide top cover, and it lost three Ki-43s and their pilots (nine-kill ace Lt Hiroshi Takiguchi, Sgt Maj Kyugo Kataoka and Sgt Hayashi Nakamura, who had claimed the unit's first victory in the Philippines) to P-38s.

The same evening, the 20th Sentai's 18 Ki-43-IIs arrived at Fabrica to join the battle over Leyte. Most of its pilots were young and inexperienced, with no more than 100 hours' flying time. Indeed, four of them had logged their first hours in the Ki-43 during the flight from Taipei. As soon as they arrived in-theatre, they were ordered to cover the convoy.

Inexperienced many of the pilots may have been, but the 2nd and 4th Air Divisions decided to deploy their full fighter strength to cover the 1st Infantry Division. There was, however, a leavening of experienced men, among them Capt Kiyoshi Namai of the 33rd Sentai. He had 12 aerial victories to his credit, and had fought over China, Burma, New Guinea and the Philippines. Namai's sentai had lost most of its strength in New Guinea during April 1944, and only seven of its pilots had survived. But by the end of August the 33rd was restored to full strength with 24 pilots and 37 Ki-43-IIIs. On 29 October it moved to Nielson airfield, and on 1 November the sentai transferred to Fabrica to cover the convoy.

That day the JAAF lost five fighters in the air and 32 on the ground at Bacolod airfield. P-38s also raided Fabrica and destroyed ten Ki-43s of the 24th and 204th Sentais, further depleting the number available for the next day's top cover mission. Nevertheless, eight Ki-43s of the 33rd,

led by Capt Namai, took off at dawn on the 2nd to provide the first watch over the beach. Five of the pilots were experiencing their first operation. Patrolling at 13,000 ft, Namai sighted two P-38s below him. Lt Bill Huisman and 2Lt Melvin Hanisch of the 9th FS had become separated from other Lightnings in the 49th FG during a fighter sweep over the area. They reported being jumped by seven 'Zeros' at 6000 ft. Namai recalled the ensuing battle;

'Two P-38s were just below us. I felt that they were too low. I made a shallow dive towards them, waving my wings to prepare my pilots for combat. I signalled to my wingman that we were going to attack. In my first pass my guns failed to fire. I zoomed away to check them and dived back to attack. The P-38 wingman banked to left so as to avoid me. I followed him, nevertheless, and fired from 220 yards. I saw my tracers hit his aircraft. The P-38 dived, trailing fuel, and then disappeared. I switched targets, but a Ki-43 flew in front of the other P-38 as I approached it and the latter instantly shot it down in flames. He was one of the newcomers, Sgt Seno. But in the next moment the Ki-43 of the second flight leader destroyed the P-38.'

2Lt Hanisch was shot down and Lt Huisman's aircraft was badly damaged after he claimed to have destroyed two 'Zeros'. The 33rd Sentai was credited with downing two P-38s for the loss of one Ki-43.

2 November also saw the 20th Sentai experience its first taste of aerial combat in the Philippines when seven Ki-43s, led by CO Maj Hideo Muraoka, took off from Fabrica airfield to fly the second watch over the convoy carrying the 1st Infantry Division. Over Ormoc Bay, Muraoka split his formation into several groups ready for combat. To the east he sighted several small black dots at the same altitude. He climbed to seize the advantage, and duly attacked 12 P-38s when they passed below his formation. Muraoka fired at a Lightning and then broke away, before climbing for the next attack. When he glanced back he saw all of his pilots chasing P-38s, which were diving to escape them. This left the sentai commander to provide the top cover for the transport vessels on his own.

His lone Ki-43 was sighted by five P-38s flying over the bay at 16,000 ft. Three of the US fighters dived on what they thought would be an easy

This Ki-43-III, possibly from the 20th Sentai, was found abandoned on Okinawa by invading US forces in April 1945. Fitted with an underwing drop tank, it may well have escaped from the Philippines earlier that month. The final production variant of the 'Oscar', the Ki-43-III was widely used by sentais tasked with defending the Philippines (*Yasuho Izawa*)

Maj Hideo Muraoka was the 20th Sentai's CO from October 1944 through to war's end. An experienced fighter pilot, he achieved a victory over P-38s during the unit's first combat in the Philippines on 2 November 1944 (*Yasuho Izawa*)

kill, but Muraoka was an old hand, and he patiently waited until the P-38s were within range. He then turned tightly in his agile Ki-43, and a stream of tracers passed over it. Muraoka challenged one of the P-38s in a head-on duel, but his aircraft was badly hit before he could open fire – he managed to nurse his crippled Ki-43 home.

Once back at base, the sentai commander found that his men had already landed to report that Lt Tanake was missing, but that they had accounted for two P-38s. Muraoka raged at them, 'You're stupid. Who was to provide the top cover?' Examination of his damaged fighter revealed that it had taken a bullet strike close to the pilot's head, with another near the fuel tank. Three P-38s had been lost, and the surviving USAAF pilots reported that they had been ambushed by a swarm of Ki-43s when they attempted to catch the single aircraft.

But these successes were the exception, for on 4 November the 20th and 33rd Sentais lost most of their Ki-43s on the ground to strafing F6Fs. The unit's personnel were therefore obliged to return to Nielson by ship and transport aircraft. The 33rd was re-equipped with more Ki-43s and re-located to Legaspi airfield to continue the cover mission.

On the same day that the 33rd had lost most of its aircraft, the 54th Sentai arrived at Zablan, near Manila, from Tokorozawa.

Fully re-equipped, the 33rd headed for Legaspi on 8 November in heavy rain, but the sentai lost its veteran CO, Maj Isao Fukuchi, en route. Capt Namai was placed in temporary command, and he claimed a P-38 on the 11th – one of four kills credited to the sentai, for the loss of a single Ki-43, on this date. By then the 54th Sentai had been brought up to the frontline at Manapla, and the 31st Sentai had returned to Luzon after being issued with more Ki-43s. These units had replaced the 204th, which had been sent back to Japan after losing 17 of its 30 pilots in just a month. The 54th made its combat debut on 11 November, claiming five kills whilst protecting the latest Leyte-bound convoy. However, the unit was bounced by F6Fs and five pilots were killed, including the sentai CO.

One of Capt Namai's first duties as deputy CO of the 33rd Sentai was to order seven of his pilots to provide an escort for *Banda-Tai* – the initial JAAF suicide attack on the 12th. The seven Ki-43s, together with four from the 24th Chutai (Independent Flying Company), joined up with the four Ki-48 suicide attackers at 0500 hrs over Legaspi, and three US ships were subsequently hit. As Namai turned to lead his fighters home, they were jumped from behind by P-38s. He was reluctant to engage them because of a shortage of fuel, and Cpl Watanabe's Ki-43 failed to return from the mission.

In late November the Japanese Supreme Command hastily planned a second general offensive on Leyte which was to follow after the landing of paratroops on 6 December (the troop transports would be escorted by 30 Ki-43s). The JAAF would be required to attack Allied positions from the air so as to soften them up prior to the counterattack commencing. This task would fall to the 2nd Flying Division in Negros, which had eight fighter sentais assigned to it. Three of these (24th, 31st and 54th) shared 34 Ki-43s between them. Five 'Oscars' were downed between 25-29 November escorting bombers or attempting to repel Allied 'heavies'.

The 25th had also seen the 20th Sentai ordered to escort two more *Banda-Tai* Ki-48s, but they were caught on the ground at Caloocan airfield by F6Fs. Two Ki-48s and 11 Ki-43s were destroyed and all the other 'Oscars' on the base damaged. A further attempt the following day was thwarted by P-38s, when three of the five Ki-43 *Yasukuni-Tai* suicide attackers were forced to make crash-landings. On the 27th, nine *Hakkou-Tai* Ki-43s, escorted by 12 others, attacked the Allied fleet in the Gulf of Leyte. These missions continued into December.

On the first day of the new month the 24th Sentai was withdrawn from the action. Having lost 12 aircraft in just a month, its place was hastily filled by the 13th Sentai and its 27 brand new Ki-43-IIIs.

24th Sentai ace WO Mitsuo Ogura initially saw action over the Philippines at the very start of the war in the Pacific. He failed to score any kills during this period, however, and it was not until the unit had transitioned from Ki-27s to Ki-43s that he began to build up his tally of successes. Ogura claimed his first victory in China in the summer of 1942, before scoring heavily in New Guinea in 1943-44. In October 1944 the 24th Sentai was posted to Fabrica, on Negros Island, and Ogura undertook a number of convoy patrols, but failed to add to his tally of 16 kills. He finished the war flying missions with the unit from its base on Formosa, where this photograph was taken (*Yasuho Izawa*)

On 4 December two Ki-43s escorted a *Banda-Tai* Ki-48 but one failed to return. The 20th Sentai also provided escorts for suicide attackers on the 5th, 7th, 10th and 15th – missions that cost the unit all the Ki-43s involved. The survivors were withdrawn to Taiwan on 22 December, by which time the number of unit personnel had decreased by a third.

With the new offensive having failed, Japanese forces now found themselves on the retreat throughout the Philippines. With very few airworthy Ki-43s left in-theatre, most sentais were pulled back to Japan. Remnants of the 30th, 31st and 54th Sentais fought on from Luzon in the new year, and on the 7th, veteran Ki-43 pilot WO Akira Sugimoto of the latter unit was involved in a legendary combat with the second-ranking American ace of World War 2.

That morning, four P-38s from the 475th FG, led by group operations officer Maj Thomas B McGuire, took off on an unauthorised sweep over Negros island. The mission's purpose was to boost McGuire's combat score. At that time his tally stood at 38 kills – just two behind 40-victory ace Maj Richard Bong, who had since returned to the US.

Approaching the Japanese base of Manapta, the P-38s were confronted by a lone Ki-43, which immediately engaged them. It was Sugimoto. He attacked McGuire's wingman, Capt Edwin Weaver, and trying to manoeuvre behind Sugimoto just above the treetops, the P-38 ace's fighter, still carrying its nearly-full external long-range fuel tanks, snap-rolled onto its back and crashed into the jungle. Lt Douglas Thropp then caught Sugimoto and fired at his aircraft, damaging it sufficiently for the Japanese pilot to make a forced landing a few miles from the wreckage of McGuire's P-38. Sugimoto was then killed in the cockpit of his Ki-43 by Filipino partisans.

Following the US invasion of Lingayen two days later, the only fighter unit to remain on nearby Luzon was the 30th Sentai. The 31st was also operable on Negros, and these two units continued to fly sporadic missions against US airfields until early April. All surviving aircraft were then withdrawn to Formosa. The groundcrews could not be evacuated, however, and some 12,000 fought on alongside their Army colleagues. Only a handful survived to war's end.

APPENDICES

Ki-43 Hayabusa Aces

Rank	Name	Unit(s)	Score
MSgt	Satoshi Anabuki	50th Sentai	39
WO	Isamu Sasaki	50th Sentai	38
Maj	Yasuhiko Kuroe	59th Sentai	30 (2)
		47th Dokuritsu Hiko Chutai	
		64th Sentai	
2Lt	Chiyoji Saito	24th Sentai	28 (21)*
Lt	Goichi Sumino	64th Sentai	27*
Lt	Moritsugu Kanai	25th Sentai	26 (7)
Lt	Isamu Hosono	25th Sentai	26 (21)*
Capt	Tomoari Hasegawa	11th Sentai	22 (19)
WO	Katsuaki Kira	24th Sentai	21 (9)
WO	Naoharu Shiromoto	11th Sentai	21 (11)
		1st Sentai	
Capt	Saburo Nakamura	64th Sentai	20* official
Capt	Nakakazu Ozaki	25th Sentai	19* official
WO	Yojiro Ohbusa	50th Sentai	19
Capt	Shogo Takeuchi	64th Sentai	19*
		68th Sentai	
WO	Bun-ichi Yamaguchi	204th Sentai	19
Lt Col	Tateo Kato	64th Sentai	18 (10)* official
WO	Kazuo Shimizu	59th Sentai	18
WO	Haruo Takagaki	11th Sentai	17 (15)*
Maj	Kiyoshi Namai	33rd Sentai	16
Lt	Tameyoshi Kuroki	33rd Sentai	16 (3)
WO	Misao Inoue	13th Sentai	16 (8)*
Sgt Maj	Yukio Shimokawa	50th Sentai	16
WO	Mitsuo Ogura	24th Sentai	16
Sgt	Tomesaku Igarashi	50th Sentai	16*
Capt	Shigeo Nango	59th Sentai	15*
Maj	Toshio Sakagawa	25th Sentai	15*
		47th Dokuritsu Hiko Chutai	
WO	Iwataro Hazawa	25th Sentai	15*
WO	Eiji Seino	25th Sentai	15
Sgt Maj	Kyushiro Ohtake	25th Sentai	15
2Lt	Masatoshi Masuzawa	1st Sentai	15 (10)
Capt	Hiroshi Onozaki	59th Sentai	14
WO	Noboru Mune	50th Sentai	14*
Sgt	Tadashi Shono	25th Sentai	14*
WO	Tokuyasu Ishizuka	11th Sentai	14 (12)
Sgt Maj	Tomio Hirohata	59th Sentai	14*
Capt	Yoshiro Kuwabara	77th Sentai	13* official
WO	Takeo Takahashi	11th Sentai	13*
2Lt	Norio Shindo	64th Sentai	13
Maj	Toyoki Eto	64th Sentai	12 (2) official
Capt	Katsumi Anma	64th Sentai	12 (5)*

Rank	Name	Unit(s)	Score
Maj	Yohei Hinoki	64th Sentai	12
Sgt	Toshimi Ikezawa	64th Sentai	12
2Lt	Yutaka Aoyagi	11th Sentai	12 (10)*
Lt Col	Mitsugu Sawada	1st Sentai	11 (7)*
Capt	Hironojo Shishimoto	11th Sentai	11
Maj	Hideo Miyabe	64th Sentai	10
WO	Kosuke Tsubone	64th Sentai	10
WO	Yoshito Yasuda	64th Sentai	10
		246th Sentai	
Maj	Yoshio Hirose	64th Sentai	9 (2)* official
Capt	Shigeru Nakazaki	50th Sentai	9*
WO	Takeomi Hayashi	59th Sentai	9 (2)
WO	Takeshi Shimizu	64th Sentai	9 (3) PoW
WO	Shokichi Omori	64th Sentai	9
Lt	Hiroshi Takiguchi	204th Sentai	9*
Capt	Takashi Tsuchiya	25th Sentai	8*
2Lt	Teizo Kanamaru	50th Sentai	8 (4) official
Maj	Koki Kawamoto	50th Sentai	8
Sgt Maj	Mitsuo Yamato	33rd Sentai	8
Lt	Naoyuki Ito	64th Sentai	8
WO	Tadao Tashiro	25th Sentai	8
Capt	Masao Miyamaru	50th Sentai	8*
WO	Yoshinori Noguchi	26th Sentai	6*
Lt	Hiroshi Gomi	204th Sentai	7*
Sgt	Miyoshi Watanabe	64th Sentai	7*

Note

The number of victories shown in some cases includes shared and probable kills

Key

official – official number of victories recognised by the JAAF
() – victories in Nomonhan Incident
* – killed in action
PoW – Prisoner of War

COLOUR PLATES

1

Ki-43-I of the 64th Sentai, flown by Maj Tateo Kato, Palembang, Sumatra, February 1942

This aircraft displays the sentai's arrowhead insignia, which was painted in different colours according to chutai assignment – white for the 1st Chutai, red with a white outline for the 2nd Chutai and yellow with a white outline for 3rd Chutai. Aircraft of the sentai HQ flight displayed a cobalt blue insignia, while the marking worn by the sentai commander's aircraft, seen here, was applied in white, with a thin blue outline. A similarly-coloured band was also added behind the cockpit. Unlike most JAAF fighter sentai COs, Maj Kato forbade his pilots from adorning their aircraft with victory symbols.

2

Ki-43-I of the 64th Sentai/2nd Chutai, flown by Capt Masuzo Ohtani, Chiang Mai, Thailand, March 1942

This aircraft displays a white band (*Senchi Hyoushiki*) on i ts rear fuselage, denoting that it was being operated by a frontline unit, while the slanting white line indicates the Ki-43's assignment to a chutai leader. 2nd Chutai leader Capt Tadao Takayama became the sentai's first casualty of the Greater East Asian War when he was killed in action on 22 December 1941. His successor, Capt Masuzo Ohtani, also perished in combat on 5 December 1942 when he was shot down over Chittagong by a Mohawk IV whilst flying this very aircraft – he had downed a Curtiss fighter just minutes earlier. By the time the next chutai leader was appointed, the unit had re-equipped with Ki-43-IIs.

3

Ki-43-I of the 64th Sentai/2nd Chutai, flown by Lt Saburo Nakamura, Mingaladon, Burma, early December 1942

The yellow slanting band with thin (text continues on page 93)

All drawings on this page are of
a Ki-43-II Hayabusa, and are to
1/48th scale, as are the drawings
overleaf

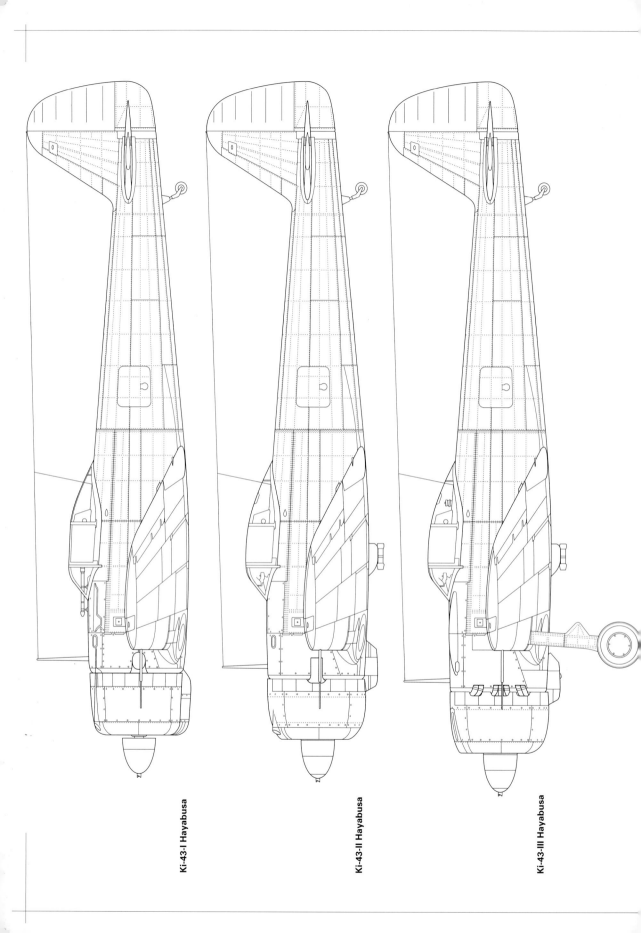

Ki-43-I Hayabusa

Ki-43-II Hayabusa

Ki-43-III Hayabusa

white outline worn by this aircraft denotes its assignment to a chutai deputy leader. Future 20-kill ace Lt Nakamura shot down two Mohawk IVs in this Ki-43 on 10 November 1942. He became 2nd Chutai deputy leader in early December following the death of Capt Ohtani.

4
Ki-43-I of the 50th Sentai/3rd Chutai, flown by Sgt Satoshi Anabuki and Lt Shigeru Nakazaki, Toungoo, Burma, January 1943

Every 50th Sentai Ki-43 displayed a name in Kanji characters at the base of its rudder. This aircraft was christened *Fubuki* ('Snowstorm') by its pilot, Sgt Satoshi Anabuki, who was to become the JAAF's leading Ki-43 ace. He called himself *Hakushoku Denko Sento Anabuki* ('White Lightning Fighter Anabuki'), and he painted three victory roundels on this fin of this machine to denote a P-40 he claimed on 25 October 1942 (his first kill in this aircraft) and a pair of Hurricanes destroyed on 18 January 1943. Fellow ace Lt Shigeru Nakazaki also regularly flew this aircraft, and nine of the roundels seen here denoted his successes prior to his death in another Ki-43-I on 23 January 1943. All aircraft assigned to the 50th Sentai displayed the lightning insignia in chutai colours – red for the 1st, yellow with a white outline for the 2nd and white for the 3rd.

5
Ki-43-II of the 64th Sentai, flown by Capt Yasuhiko Kuroe, Toungoo, Burma, March 1943

This aircraft is depicted as it appeared when flown by high-scoring JAAF ace Capt Kuroe, who was placed in temporary command of the 64th Sentai in February 1943 after it lost two COs in combat in the space of just a fortnight. Maj Masami Yagi was shot down by a Mohawk IV on the 12th (in the first combat by the 64th with the Ki-43-II), and his successor, Maj Takeyo Akera, died on the 25th whilst dogfighting with P-40Es. Kuroe, who had been leader of the 3rd Chutai since April 1942, commanded the sentai until Maj Yoshio Hirose (known as the best shot in the JAAF) arrived in March. Kuroe then became the 64th's executive officer through to December 1943. Note the fighter's cobalt blue insignia, denoting its assignment to a pilot from the sentai HQ.

6
Ki-43-II of the 50th Sentai/2nd Chutai, flown by Capt Masao Miyamaru, Toungoo, Burma, May 1943

This aircraft displays the name *Myo or Tae* ('Outstanding Skill') in Kanji characters. Note also that the leading edge of its engine cowling and propeller spinner have been painted in the 2nd Chutai's yellow colour of the period. Eight-victory ace Capt Miyamaru was transferred to the Akeno Fighter School in August 1943 after having led the 50th's 2nd Chutai from February 1942, and he was killed whilst flying a Ki-84 Hayate of the 200th Sentai in the defence of the Philippines on 29 October 1944.

7
Ki-43-II of the 64th Sentai/2nd Chutai, flown by Sgt Miyoshi Watanabe, Toungoo, Burma, March-April 1943

This aircraft displays the camouflage paint scheme it wore when allocated to 2nd Chutai seven-kill ace Sgt Miyoshi Watanabe. Personal markings and individual victory tallies on

aircraft were officially forbidden in the JAAF, and this rule was rigorously enforced within the 64th Sentai, which considered unit cohesion to be of greater importance than individual display. Capt Kuroe spoke about this directive at length in his wartime diary.

8
Ki-43-II of the 64th Sentai/3rd Chutai, flown by Lt Yohei Hinoki, Mingaladon, Burma, November 1943

This fighter displays the typical mid- to late-war camouflage scheme applied to Ki-43-II/IIIs in Burma by the 64th Sentai. The last 'Oscar' assigned to Lt Yohei Hinoki, this fighter had originally been flown by chutai leader Capt Kuroe. However, he passed it on to Lt Takeshi Endo when he became temporary CO of the 64th in March 1943. Endo was killed in another 'Oscar' on 15 May over Kunming, and Hinoki inherited this aircraft when he became the new 3rd Chutai leader. Noteworthy is its spinner painted in the 3rd Chutai colours. Hinoki downed a P-51A in this machine on 25 November, although he suffered grievous wounds that resulted in him losing his right leg whilst battling more Mustangs two days later. It is possible that he was flying this veteran Ki-43-II at the time.

9
Ki-43-III of the 64th Sentai/1st Chutai, flown by Sgt Toshimi Ikezawa, Meiktila, Burma, November 1944

Although assigned to a 12-victory ace, this aircraft strictly adheres to the 64th Sentai's no personal markings rule. Indeed, the 1st Chutai's white arrow is the only embellishment of note. Ki-43-IIIs started to reach the 64th Sentai at Meiktila in September 1944, and they were operated alongside Model IIs until war's end.

10
Ki-43-III of the 64th Sentai, flown by Maj Hideo Miyabe, Kurakore, Indochina, May 1945

This aircraft displays the sentai commander's fuselage band similar to that worn by Maj Kato's Ki-43-I three years earlier. The kanju character on the tail of this machine reads *Aso*, after Mount Aso of Miyabe's native prefecture in Japan. The last CO of the 64th, Miyabe ended the war with at least ten aerial victories to his name.

11
Ki-43-I of the 24th Sentai/2nd Chutai, Canton, China, July 1942

This aircraft features the highly stylised '24' insignia worn on the tails of all Ki-43s assigned to the sentai – these were applied in typical chutai colours of white for the 1st, red for the 2nd and yellow for the 3rd. These fighters in their unpainted silver finish represented the first opponents encountered by Allied P-40 pilots in China during July 1942. The JAAF ordered the unit to apply Hinomarus (the rising-sun national marking) to the fuselage sides of its Ki-43s in October 1942.

12
Ki-43-I of the 10th Dokuritsu Hiko Chutai (10th Independent Flying Chutai), Canton, China, August 1942

This aircraft was operated by one of the oldest JAAF fighter units in China. The 10th Independent Flying Chutai had been fighting here since September 1931, and it was re-formed as the 25th Sentai following enlargement in November 1942. Initially, the latter unit was comprised of only two chutais, and the markings displayed by its aircraft followed the practice established by its predecessor – horizontal bands on the tail in white for the 1st Chutai and red for the 2nd.

13

Ki-43-II of the 25th Sentai/2nd Chutai, flown by Capt Nakakazu Ozaki, Hankow, China, summer 1943

With the arrival of Ki-43-IIs in China in May 1943, the 25th Sentai revised its unit marking by replacing its horizontal band with a bold slanting stripe in chutai colours on the fin. Aircraft now also featured their individual numbers in white on the tail. This well weathered aircraft was assigned to high-scoring ace, and 2nd Chutai leader, Capt Nakakazu Ozaki for much of 1943.

14

Ki-43-II of the 33rd Sentai/2nd Chutai, flown by Capt Kiyoshi Namai, Hanoi, Indochina, September 1943

This fighter displays the chutai leader's red band around its rear fuselage. Namai fought in China, Burma, New Guinea and the Philippines, where he was placed in temporary command of the sentai when the CO, Maj Hiroshi Yamaura, was killed. Namai, who was the 33rd's joint ranking ace with 16 confirmed aerial victories and eight probables, survived the war.

15

Ki-43-II of the 25th Sentai/2nd Chutai, flown by Sgt Maj Kyushiro Ohtake, Hankow, China, December 1943

This aircraft was delivered to the 25th in China in silver factory finish, over which camouflage paint was liberally applied. By December 1943, following six months of frontline operations, dark green had worn off. Ohtake, who served exclusively with the unit in China, had excellent eyesight, and he was renowned for his ability to spot the enemy first.

16

Ki-43-II of the 25th Sentai, flown by Maj Toshio Sakagawa, Hankow, late 1943

This fighter displays a rare three-tone camouflage scheme, as well as a triple-colour tail marking and '00' individual number. The latter two features indicate its assignment to sentai CO, and 15-kill ace, Maj Toshio Sakagawa, who led the 25th for more than 18 months. Regarded within the JAAF as an outstanding commander, he was CO of 47th Dokuritsu Hiko Chutai, which was an experimental unit equipped with the pre-production Ki-44s. He was appointed CO of the newly-established 25th Sentai in November 1942 and remained in command until July 1944. During this time he scored the majority of his 15 victories, including three P-51B/Cs (possibly in this aircraft) on 25 May 1944 over Hankow.

17

Ki-43-II of the 25th Sentai/2nd Chutai, flown by Sgt Maj Iwataro Hazawa, Hankow, China, spring 1944

This fighter was allocated to one of the JAAF's boldest aces, Sgt Maj Iwataro Hazawa, who received a special citation from 5th Air Force CO Lt Gen Shimoyama in August 1944. Having claimed 15 victories, Hazawa was killed in action on 14 January 945 when his parachute failed to open after he baled out of s blazing fighter over Hankow airfield.

18

Ki-43-II of the 25th Sentai/3rd Chutai flown by Capt Keisaku Motohashi, Hankow, China, spring 1944

This aircraft displays the yellow band outlined in white, denoting the fighter's assigment to the 3rd Chutai. The 25th was reinforced by the addition of a third chutai in November 1943, with Capt Motohashi serving as its first leader. He was killed over central China on 4 August 1944 while leading his three Ki-43s against four P-40Ns of the USAAF's 26th FS.

19

Ki-43-II of the 25th Sentai/2nd Chutai, flown by Cpl Haruyuki Todai, Hankow, China, spring 1944

The 25th Sentai represented an exception to the general JAAF rule stating that all frontline fighters had to display a white Senti Hyoushiki band on their rear fuselages. Todai participated in numerous battles with P-38s of the 449th FS in the early months of 1944, serving as Capt Motohashi's wingman for much of this time. During one such clash the two 'Oscar' pilots succeeded in damaging three of their assailants without loss. Two of the P-38s were subsequently forced to make emergency landings prior to making it home.

20

Ki-43-III of the 25th Sentai/1st Chutai, flown by Sgt Goro Miyamoto, Hengyang, China, November 1944

This 'Oscar' was one of the first Ki-43-IIIs to reach the 25th Sentai in China, the unit operating the final Hayabusa variant for just four months prior to switching to the Ki-84. The aircraft's pilot, Sgt Miyamoto, had joined the 25th 12 months earlier. Just weeks later, on 10 December, he claimed to have shot down a P-51 over Kiukang. This would have given the Ki-43 its first Mustang kill in China. However, no corroborating evidence has yet been discovered in Allied records to support Miyamoto's claim.

21

Ki-43-III of the 48th Sentai/1st Chutai, flown by Sgt Sou Okabe, Nanking, China, August 1945

This aircraft displays the sentai's stylised '48' insignia in white on its tail. Note that the propeller spinner has also been painted in the chutai colour. The pilot's nickname *Abe* appears just forward of the tail in kanji characters. The 48th Sentai failed to produce a single Ki-43 ace primarily because the unit was stuck with Ki-27s until January 1944.

22

Ki-43-I of the 11th Sentai, flown by Maj Katsuji Sugiura, Mingaladon, Burma, November 1942

The two bold white bands behind this aircraft's cockpit indicate that this garish Ki-43-I (featuring lightning bolts in all three chutai colours on the tail) was assigned to the sentai CO, Maj Katsuji Sugiura. He led the unit, known as the 'Lightning Sentai', from March 1942 until he was killed in action on 6 February 1943 in New Guinea.

23

Ki-43-I of the 1st Sentai/1st Chutai, Akeno Fighter School, Japan, July 1942

The bands around the rear fuselage of this fighter indicate the flight (2nd Flight) that was operating it, while the rudder bands display the aircraft's numerical position within its chutai. The red colour indicates the Ki-43's assignment to the 1st Chutai.

24

Ki-43-II of the 59th Sentai/2nd Chutai, flown by Capt Shigeo Nango, But, New Guinea, September 1943
The 59th's initial sentai insignia incorporated a lightning bolt on the fuselage, which was then reduced in size and moved to the tail. This was eventually changed to the slanting tail band in appropriate chutai colours as seen here. Nango, who claimed 15 victories, was 2nd Chutai leader and then sentai XO.

25

Ki-43-II of the 59th Sentai/3rd Chutai, flown by Sgt Maj Tomio Hirohata, But, New Guinea, October 1943
This aircraft displays a rare personal marking on its fuselage. Hirohata was trained in the art of air combat in 1940 by Capt Yasuikio Kuroe, and he went on to claim 14 victories prior to his death in a flying accident in Japan on 22 April 1945.

26

Ki-43-II of the 63rd Sentai/1st Chutai, Wewak, New Guinea, early 1944
This aircraft features the sentai's '63' insignia in white, indicating its assignment to the 1st Chutai. This unit existed for just over a year, and flew Ki-43s in New Guinea from December 1943 until it was wiped out with the fall of Hollandia in April 1944. Enjoying only modest success in combat, and producing no aces, the sentai's leading pilots were Capt Tomio Matsumoto, who claimed four P-38s destroyed on 18 January over Wewak prior to being shot down and killed in the same mission, and Lt Hiroshi Endo, whose 3rd Chutai claimed 10+ victories in as many engagements. The latter subsequently died of sickness in-theatre.

27

Ki-43-II of the 248th Sentai/2nd Chutai, Hollandia, New Guinea, March 1944
The aircraft displays the distinctive sentai insignia derived from the leaf of the Ashi (reed), which acknowledges the name of the 248th's home airfield of Ashiya. Noteworthy is the way the points of the leaves indicate the numbers two, four and eight. The chutai colours were white for the 1st, red for the 2nd and yellow for the 3rd. Formed in August 1942 and initially equipped with Ki-27s, the 248th was posted to New Guinea in October 1943 and fought on until disbanded following the Allied capture of Hollandia in April 1944. Although the sentai claimed 97 aircraft shot down or damaged in New Guinea, it failed to produced a single ace. It also lost 24 pilots in aerial combat and most of its remaining personnel during the retreat from Hollandia.

28

Ki-43-II of the 77th Sentai/2nd Chutai, flown by Capt Yoshihide Matsuo, Wewak, New Guinea, June 1944
This aircraft displays the horizontal arrow sentai insignia derived from the number 7. Chutai colours were white with a thin cobalt blue outline for the 1st Chutai, blue with a white outline for the 2nd and red with a white outline for the 3rd. Having seen considerable combat with the Ki-27 in China pre-war and then in Burma between December 1941 and June 1942, the 77th converted to Ki-43-IIs in August 1943. Briefly returning to Burma in January-February 1944, the sentai was transferred to New Guinea and wiped out at Hollandia. Capt Yoshihide Matsuo served as the 3rd Chutai leader from October 1942 until he was killed in combat on the ground in western New Guinea in June 1944.

29

Ki-43-II of the 20th Sentai/1st Chutai, Hsiaochiang, Formosa, October 1944
The aircraft displays the '20' sentai insignia in red and yellow on its tail. The propeller spinner is painted in the 1st Chutai's white. A number of Formosa-based Ki-43-IIs were painted in this distinctive blue with silver undersides. Formed in December 1943, the 20th enjoyed a relatively quiet war until sent to the Philippines from Formosa in October 1944. Losing most of its aircraft and many of its pilots in combat, the sentai retreated to Formosa in December. Between March and June 1945, 24 of its pilots undertook suicide attacks on Allied vessels off Okinawa.

30

Ki-43-III of the 33rd Sentai/3rd Chutai, flown by Lt Hitoshi Yamamoto, Legaspi, Luzon, the Philippines, November 1944
This aircraft displays the 3rd Chutai's yellow colour, outlined in white. The 33rd Sentai re-equipped with Model IIIs at Legaspi in November 1944, although it suffered terrible losses prior to evacuating to Betung, in Sumatra, in January 1945. The pilot of this aircraft, Lt Hitoshi Yamamoto, received a 'Military Exploits' badge from 4th Air Force CO Lt Gen Tominaga at Legaspi on 21 November 1944.

31

Ki-43-II of the 54th Sentai/3rd Chutai, flown by WO Akira Sugimoto, Fabrica, Negros Island, the Philippines, January 1945
This aircraft displays the sentai insignia consisting of an *Orizuru* design (the figure of a crane folded from paper), its application in yellow denoting that its assignment to the 3rd Chutai (white was for the 1st and red for the 2nd). Having been an instructor for several years, Sugimoto was one of the most experienced Ki-43 pilots in the Philippines by early 1945. On 7 January, he engaged four P-38s, led by 38-kill ace Maj Thomas McGuire, over Negros Island in this aircraft. In the subsequent battle with the lone Ki-43, McGuire lost control of his aircraft and crashed to his death. Sugimoto was then attacked by Lt Douglas Thropp, and sufficient damage was caused to his fighter to necessitate a forced landing near to where McGuire had crashed. Having survived the crash, Akira Sugimoto was slain in the cockpit of his 'Oscar' by Filipino partisans.

32

Ki-43-III of the 204th Sentai, flown by Capt Hiroshi Murakami, Hualien, Formosa, July 1945
This sentai's modest insignia appeared in white on aircraft of the 1st Chutai, red for the 2nd and yellow for the 3rd. Having seen action in the Philippines in October-November 1944, the unit re-equipped with Ki-43-IIIs in Japan and was then posted to Indochina. The 204th finished the conflict in Formosa. Murakami was sentai CO from January 1945 until war's end.

INDEX

References to illustrations are shown in **bold**. Plates are shown with page and caption locators in brackets.

white outline worn by this aircraft denotes its assignment to a chutai deputy leader. Future 20-kill ace Lt Nakamura shot down two Mohawk IVs in this Ki-43 on 10 November 1942. He became 2nd Chutai deputy leader in early December following the death of Capt Ohtani.

4
Ki-43-I of the 50th Sentai/3rd Chutai, flown by Sgt Satoshi Anabuki and Lt Shigeru Nakazaki, Toungoo, Burma, January 1943

Every 50th Sentai Ki-43 displayed a name in Kanji characters at the base of its rudder. This aircraft was christened *Fubuki* ('Snowstorm') by its pilot, Sgt Satoshi Anabuki, who was to become the JAAF's leading Ki-43 ace. He called himself *Hakushoku Denko Sento Anabuki* ('White Lightning Fighter Anabuki'), and he painted three victory roundels on this fin of this machine to denote a P-40 he claimed on 25 October 1942 (his first kill in this aircraft) and a pair of Hurricanes destroyed on 18 January 1943. Fellow ace Lt Shigeru Nakazaki also regularly flew this aircraft, and nine of the roundels seen here denoted his successes prior to his death in another Ki-43-I on 23 January 1943. All aircraft assigned to the 50th Sentai displayed the lightning insignia in chutai colours – red for the 1st, yellow with a white outline for the 2nd and white for the 3rd.

5
Ki-43-II of the 64th Sentai, flown by Capt Yasuhiko Kuroe, Toungoo, Burma, March 1943

This aircraft is depicted as it appeared when flown by high-scoring JAAF ace Capt Kuroe, who was placed in temporary command of the 64th Sentai in February 1943 after it lost two COs in combat in the space of just a fortnight. Maj Masami Yagi was shot down by a Mohawk IV on the 12th (in the first combat by the 64th with the Ki-43-II), and his successor, Maj Takeyo Akera, died on the 25th whilst dogfighting with P-40Es. Kuroe, who had been leader of the 3rd Chutai since April 1942, commanded the sentai until Maj Yoshio Hirose (known as the best shot in the JAAF) arrived in March. Kuroe then became the 64th's executive officer through to December 1943. Note the fighter's cobalt blue insignia, denoting its assignment to a pilot from the sentai HQ.

6
Ki-43-II of the 50th Sentai/2nd Chutai, flown by Capt Masao Miyamaru, Toungoo, Burma, May 1943

This aircraft displays the name *Myo or Tae* ('Outstanding Skill') in Kanji characters. Note also that the leading edge of its engine cowling and propeller spinner have been painted in the 2nd Chutai's yellow colour of the period. Eight-victory ace Capt Miyamaru was transferred to the Akeno Fighter School in August 1943 after having led the 50th's 2nd Chutai from February 1942, and he was killed whilst flying a Ki-84 Hayate of the 200th Sentai in the defence of the Philippines on 29 October 1944.

7
Ki-43-II of the 64th Sentai/2nd Chutai, flown by Sgt Miyoshi Watanabe, Toungoo, Burma, March-April 1943

This aircraft displays the camouflage paint scheme it wore when allocated to 2nd Chutai seven-kill ace Sgt Miyoshi Watanabe. Personal markings and individual victory tallies on

aircraft were officially forbidden in the JAAF, and this rule was rigorously enforced within the 64th Sentai, which considered unit cohesion to be of greater importance than individual display. Capt Kuroe spoke about this directive at length in his wartime diary.

8
Ki-43-II of the 64th Sentai/3rd Chutai, flown by Lt Yohei Hinoki, Mingaladon, Burma, November 1943

This fighter displays the typical mid- to late-war camouflage scheme applied to Ki-43-II/IIIs in Burma by the 64th Sentai. The last 'Oscar' assigned to Lt Yohei Hinoki, this fighter had originally been flown by chutai leader Capt Kuroe. However, he passed it on to Lt Takeshi Endo when he became temporary CO of the 64th in March 1943. Endo was killed in another 'Oscar' on 15 May over Kunming, and Hinoki inherited this aircraft when he became the new 3rd Chutai leader. Noteworthy is its spinner painted in the 3rd Chutai colours. Hinoki downed a P-51A in this machine on 25 November, although he suffered grievous wounds that resulted in him losing his right leg whilst battling more Mustangs two days later. It is possible that he was flying this veteran Ki-43-II at the time.

9
Ki-43-III of the 64th Sentai/1st Chutai, flown by Sgt Toshimi Ikezawa, Meiktila, Burma, November 1944

Although assigned to a 12-victory ace, this aircraft strictly adheres to the 64th Sentai's no personal markings rule. Indeed, the 1st Chutai's white arrow is the only embellishment of note. Ki-43-IIIs started to reach the 64th Sentai at Meiktila in September 1944, and they were operated alongside Model IIs until war's end.

10
Ki-43-III of the 64th Sentai, flown by Maj Hideo Miyabe, Kurakore, Indochina, May 1945

This aircraft displays the sentai commander's fuselage band similar to that worn by Maj Kato's Ki-43-I three years earlier. The kanju character on the tail of this machine reads *Aso*, after Mount Aso of Miyabe's native prefecture in Japan. The last CO of the 64th, Miyabe ended the war with at least ten aerial victories to his name.

11
Ki-43-I of the 24th Sentai/2nd Chutai, Canton, China, July 1942

This aircraft features the highly stylised '24' insignia worn on the tails of all Ki-43s assigned to the sentai – these were applied in typical chutai colours of white for the 1st, red for the 2nd and yellow for the 3rd. These fighters in their unpainted silver finish represented the first opponents encountered by Allied P-40 pilots in China during July 1942. The JAAF ordered the unit to apply Hinomarus (the rising-sun national marking) to the fuselage sides of its Ki-43s in October 1942.

12
Ki-43-I of the 10th Dokuritsu Hiko Chutai (10th Independent Flying Chutai), Canton, China, August 1942

This aircraft was operated by one of the oldest JAAF fighter units in China. The 10th Independent Flying Chutai had been fighting here since September 1931, and it was re-formed as the 25th Sentai following enlargement in November 1942. Initially, the latter unit was comprised of only two chutais, and the markings displayed by its aircraft followed the practice established by its predecessor – horizontal bands on the tail in white for the 1st Chutai and red for the 2nd.

13

Ki-43-II of the 25th Sentai/2nd Chutai, flown by Capt Nakakazu Ozaki, Hankow, China, summer 1943

With the arrival of Ki-43-IIs in China in May 1943, the 25th Sentai revised its unit marking by replacing its horizontal band with a bold slanting stripe in chutai colours on the fin. Aircraft now also featured their individual numbers in white on the tail. This well weathered aircraft was assigned to high-scoring ace, and 2nd Chutai leader, Capt Nakakazu Ozaki for much of 1943.

14

Ki-43-II of the 33rd Sentai/2nd Chutai, flown by Capt Kiyoshi Namai, Hanoi, Indochina, September 1943

This fighter displays the chutai leader's red band around its rear fuselage. Namai fought in China, Burma, New Guinea and the Philippines, where he was placed in temporary command of the sentai when the CO, Maj Hiroshi Yamaura, was killed. Namai, who was the 33rd's joint ranking ace with 16 confirmed aerial victories and eight probables, survived the war.

15

Ki-43-II of the 25th Sentai/2nd Chutai, flown by Sgt Maj Kyushiro Ohtake, Hankow, China, December 1943

This aircraft was delivered to the 25th in China in silver factory finish, over which camouflage paint was liberally applied. By December 1943, following six months of frontline operations, dark green had worn off. Ohtake, who served exclusively with the unit in China, had excellent eyesight, and he was renowned for his ability to spot the enemy first.

16

Ki-43-II of the 25th Sentai, flown by Maj Toshio Sakagawa, Hankow, late 1943

This fighter displays a rare three-tone camouflage scheme, as well as a triple-colour tail marking and '00' individual number. The latter two features indicate its assignment to sentai CO, and 15-kill ace, Maj Toshio Sakagawa, who led the 25th for more than 18 months. Regarded within the JAAF as an outstanding commander, he was CO of 47th Dokuritsu Hiko Chutai, which was an experimental unit equipped with the pre-production Ki-44s. He was appointed CO of the newly-established 25th Sentai in November 1942 and remained in command until July 1944. During this time he scored the majority of his 15 victories, including three P-51B/Cs (possibly in this aircraft) on 25 May 1944 over Hankow.

17

Ki-43-II of the 25th Sentai/2nd Chutai, flown by Sgt Maj Iwataro Hazawa, Hankow, China, spring 1944

This fighter was allocated to one of the JAAF's boldest aces, Sgt Maj Iwataro Hazawa, who received a special citation from 5th Air Force CO Lt Gen Shimoyama in August 1944. Having claimed 15 victories, Hazawa was killed in action on 14 January 1945 when his parachute failed to open after he baled out of his blazing fighter over Hankow airfield.

18

Ki-43-II of the 25th Sentai/3rd Chutai flown by Capt Keisaku Motohashi, Hankow, China, spring 1944

This aircraft displays the yellow band outlined in white, denoting the fighter's assigment to the 3rd Chutai. The 25th was reinforced by the addition of a third chutai in November 1943, with Capt Motohashi serving as its first leader. He was killed over central China on 4 August 1944 while leading his three Ki-43s against four P-40Ns of the USAAF's 26th FS.

19

Ki-43-II of the 25th Sentai/2nd Chutai, flown by Cpl Haruyuki Todai, Hankow, China, spring 1944

The 25th Sentai represented an exception to the general JAAF rule stating that all frontline fighters had to display a white Senti Hyoushiki band on their rear fuselages. Todai participated in numerous battles with P-38s of the 449th FS in the early months of 1944, serving as Capt Motohashi's wingman for much of this time. During one such clash the two 'Oscar' pilots succeeded in damaging three of their assailants without loss. Two of the P-38s were subsequently forced to make emergency landings prior to making it home.

20

Ki-43-III of the 25th Sentai/1st Chutai, flown by Sgt Goro Miyamoto, Hengyang, China, November 1944

This 'Oscar' was one of the first Ki-43-IIIs to reach the 25th Sentai in China, the unit operating the final Hayabusa variant for just four months prior to switching to the Ki-84. The aircraft's pilot, Sgt Miyamoto, had joined the 25th 12 months earlier. Just weeks later, on 10 December, he claimed to have shot down a P-51 over Kiukang. This would have given the Ki-43 its first Mustang kill in China. However, no corroborating evidence has yet been discovered in Allied records to support Miyamoto's claim.

21

Ki-43-III of the 48th Sentai/1st Chutai, flown by Sgt Sou Okabe, Nanking, China, August 1945

This aircraft displays the sentai's stylised '48' insignia in white on its tail. Note that the propeller spinner has also been painted in the chutai colour. The pilot's nickname *Abe* appears just forward of the tail in kanji characters. The 48th Sentai failed to produce a single Ki-43 ace primarily because the unit was stuck with Ki-27s until January 1944.

22

Ki-43-I of the 11th Sentai, flown by Maj Katsuji Sugiura, Mingaladon, Burma, November 1942

The two bold white bands behind this aircraft's cockpit indicate that this garish Ki-43-I (featuring lightning bolts in all three chutai colours on the tail) was assigned to the sentai CO, Maj Katsuji Sugiura. He led the unit, known as the 'Lightning Sentai', from March 1942 until he was killed in action on 6 February 1943 in New Guinea.

23

Ki-43-I of the 1st Sentai/1st Chutai, Akeno Fighter School, Japan, July 1942

The bands around the rear fuselage of this fighter indicate the flight (2nd Flight) that was operating it, while the rudder bands display the aircraft's numerical position within its chutai. The red colour indicates the Ki-43's assignment to the 1st Chutai.

24

Ki-43-II of the 59th Sentai/2nd Chutai, flown by Capt Shigeo Nango, But, New Guinea, September 1943

The 59th's initial sentai insignia incorporated a lightning bolt on the fuselage, which was then reduced in size and moved to the tail. This was eventually changed to the slanting tail band in appropriate chutai colours as seen here. Nango, who claimed 15 victories, was 2nd Chutai leader and then sentai XO.

25

Ki-43-II of the 59th Sentai/3rd Chutai, flown by Sgt Maj Tomio Hirohata, But, New Guinea, October 1943

This aircraft displays a rare personal marking on its fuselage. Hirohata was trained in the art of air combat in 1940 by Capt Yasuikio Kuroe, and he went on to claim 14 victories prior to his death in a flying accident in Japan on 22 April 1945.

26

Ki-43-II of the 63rd Sentai/1st Chutai, Wewak, New Guinea, early 1944

This aircraft features the sentai's '63' insignia in white, indicating its assignment to the 1st Chutai. This unit existed for just over a year, and flew Ki-43s in New Guinea from December 1943 until it was wiped out with the fall of Hollandia in April 1944. Enjoying only modest success in combat, and producing no aces, the sentai's leading pilots were Capt Tomio Matsumoto, who claimed four P-38s destroyed on 18 January over Wewak prior to being shot down and killed in the same mission, and Lt Hiroshi Endo, whose 3rd Chutai claimed 10+ victories in as many engagements. The latter subsequently died of sickness in-theatre.

27

Ki-43-II of the 248th Sentai/2nd Chutai, Hollandia, New Guinea, March 1944

The aircraft displays the distinctive sentai insignia derived from the leaf of the Ashi (reed), which acknowledges the name of the 248th's home airfield of Ashiya. Noteworthy is the way the points of the leaves indicate the numbers two, four and eight. The chutai colours were white for the 1st, red for the 2nd and yellow for the 3rd. Formed in August 1942 and initially equipped with Ki-27s, the 248th was posted to New Guinea in October 1943 and fought on until disbanded following the Allied capture of Hollandia in April 1944. Although the sentai claimed 97 aircraft shot down or damaged in New Guinea, it failed to produced a single ace. It also lost 24 pilots in aerial combat and most of its remaining personnel during the retreat from Hollandia.

28

Ki-43-II of the 77th Sentai/2nd Chutai, flown by Capt Yoshihide Matsuo, Wewak, New Guinea, June 1944

This aircraft displays the horizontal arrow sentai insignia derived from the number 7. Chutai colours were white with a thin cobalt blue outline for the 1st Chutai, blue with a white outline for the 2nd and red with a white outline for the 3rd. Having seen considerable combat with the Ki-27 in China pre-war and then in Burma between December 1941 and June

1942, the 77th converted to Ki-43-IIs in August 1943. Briefly returning to Burma in January-February 1944, the sentai was transferred to New Guinea and wiped out at Hollandia. Capt Yoshihide Matsuo served as the 3rd Chutai leader from October 1942 until he was killed in combat on the ground in western New Guinea in June 1944.

29

Ki-43-II of the 20th Sentai/1st Chutai, Hsiaochiang, Formosa, October 1944

The aircraft displays the '20' sentai insignia in red and yellow on its tail. The propeller spinner is painted in the 1st Chutai's white. A number of Formosa-based Ki-43-IIs were painted in this distinctive blue with silver undersides. Formed in December 1943, the 20th enjoyed a relatively quiet war until sent to the Philippines from Formosa in October 1944. Losing most of its aircraft and many of its pilots in combat, the sentai retreated to Formosa in December. Between March and June 1945, 24 of its pilots undertook suicide attacks on Allied vessels off Okinawa.

30

Ki-43-III of the 33rd Sentai/3rd Chutai, flown by Lt Hitoshi Yamamoto, Legaspi, Luzon, the Philippines, November 1944

This aircraft displays the 3rd Chutai's yellow colour, outlined in white. The 33rd Sentai re-equipped with Model IIIs at Legaspi in November 1944, although it suffered terrible losses prior to evacuating to Betung, in Sumatra, in January 1945. The pilot of this aircraft, Lt Hitoshi Yamamoto, received a 'Military Exploits' badge from 4th Air Force CO Lt Gen Tominaga at Legaspi on 21 November 1944.

31

Ki-43-II of the 54th Sentai/3rd Chutai, flown by WO Akira Sugimoto, Fabrica, Negros Island, the Philippines, January 1945

This aircraft displays the sentai insignia consisting of an *Orizuru* design (the figure of a crane folded from paper), its application in yellow denoting that its assignment to the 3rd Chutai (white was for the 1st and red for the 2nd). Having been an instructor for several years, Sugimoto was one of the most experienced Ki-43 pilots in the Philippines by early 1945. On 7 January, he engaged four P-38s, led by 38-kill ace Maj Thomas McGuire, over Negros Island in this aircraft. In the subsequent battle with the lone Ki-43, McGuire lost control of his aircraft and crashed to his death. Sugimoto was then attacked by Lt Douglas Thropp, and sufficient damage was caused to his fighter to necessitate a forced landing near to where McGuire had crashed. Having survived the crash, Akira Sugimoto was slain in the cockpit of his 'Oscar' by Filipino partisans.

32

Ki-43-III of the 204th Sentai, flown by Capt Hiroshi Murakami, Hualien, Formosa, July 1945

This sentai's modest insignia appeared in white on aircraft of the 1st Chutai, red for the 2nd and yellow for the 3rd. Having seen action in the Philippines in October-November 1944, the unit re-equipped with Ki-43-IIIs in Japan and was then posted to Indochina. The 204th finished the conflict in Formosa. Murakami was sentai CO from January 1945 until war's end.

INDEX

References to illustrations are shown in **bold**. Plates are shown with page and caption locators in brackets.